YOU CAN DO IT!

JEROME STOKES

YOU CAN DO IT!

ISBN: 0-9786581-0-8
978-0-9786581-0-6

Published by

LIFEBRIDGE
B O O K S
P.O. BOX 49428
CHARLOTTE, NC 28277

Printed in the United States of America.

CONTENTS

INTRODUCTION

What is it that you are facing at this very moment that seems insurmountable? Perhaps it is something you have been wrestling with for some time, or maybe it surfaced recently. It is bothering you and you are trying to decide how you are going to deal with it. Maybe you have evaluated the situation and it seems there is no approach which will bring it to closure. It has escalated to the point that it has now become a hindrance to your forward movement in life. You can see on the other side of the obstacle, but you cannot get past it. There may not be a desire within you to give up, but you are now starting to feel that there is nothing you can do about it. Some of you have already uttered the words of defeat, "I cannot do it!"

What is it that you want to achieve in your life? What is it that you have had both day and night visions about? What things have you allowed to cause you to feel you cannot achieve your visions?

So many people have had great plans to achieve big things in their lives, but have allowed themselves to gradually drift from the fulfillment of it because something or someone constituted a major blockage in their path. Instead of facing the challenge of the blockage and defeating it, they submit themselves to defeat because they feel that they cannot do it.

The conclusion that something cannot be achieved is a serious detriment to the life of an individual who has the ability to achieve it. It is understood that there will be some things that we cannot do. This is just a basic fact of our earthly existence. The detriment is realized or manifested when one operates far below his or her ability. They have the ability, but are not using it. This can occur when people allow themselves to arrive at the conclusion that they cannot do what they have attempted to do, because they have encountered significant opposition.

Some have the ability and don't know it. They will see that ability manifest as they proceed forward. Others have ability but allow themselves to become convinced they are functioning at the maximum level of their ability when, in actuality, they are not. Still others have the ability to achieve and know it, but lack the drive or motivation to forge forward and achieve.

It is important that we do not count ourselves out. We must not allow ourselves to operate in mindsets that promote increased hardship and failure. Instead, we must face the challenges of life with an attitude that we will meet and overcome every one. We must not allow the failures that we encounter along the way cause us to feel that we are failures personally. Instead we must remember that every great person is great, not only because of their ability to achieve, but also because of their ability to experience failure, overcome it, and go on to success.

One of the goals of this writing is to convince all who read it that they possess the necessary ability to achieve. I desire to see each reader rise to a new level of accomplishment.

The application of the principles of this book has brought me to a position of significant achievement in my life. They have impacted me to such a degree that I felt a need to share them in this book. I pray for your enlightenment, application, and achievement as you apply these principles.

— Jerome Stokes

CHAPTER 1

THE DIFFERENCE IN YOU

As a youngster, I was keenly aware of my surroundings. Our family was united and my parents provided for me and my brothers and sisters the best way they could.

Our standard of living was below middle class, but my parents worked hard and we seemed to always have provision. We lived in inner city row houses and the projects. The structures were not in the best condition and the streets were in constant need of repair.

At times, a spirit of hopelessness and despair hovered over our community. Many of the adult males worked, but were not receiving large salaries—and most earned just enough to make ends meet. Others were unemployed and some never sought work. There was a high frustration level because so many were striving to advance themselves, yet failing in their attempts.

I saw a few of my childhood friends turn to crime and end up behind bars. Those who were not sentenced to the natural jails were imprisoned by their own frustration and despair caused by the deplorable conditions they lived under. Many felt they would never rise above this economic level.

However, there were individuals who, like my parents, instilled quality traits into their children, combined with the implantation of ambition. By their guidance, I came to realize that the negative conditions would not permanently reside in my life—they were only temporary.

My thinking changed as I came to the realization I was destined to do great things and to make a difference in my immediate surroundings and the world.

Many of you are believers in Christ. The fact that the Lord saved you is a clear indication there is something special about you.

Remember, when God blesses people as He has favored us, He has extraordinary plans in mind. We have a unique purpose and assignment. To a degree, the enemy has been successful in causing believers to be unaware of the qualities that lie within them. We seem to pay more attention to our problems than to the development of the latent potential inside.

We are all too familiar with trouble and hardship. In fact, many of the sermons preached to the body of Christ are geared to talk about our struggles. While this may be necessary to aid in the deliverance of some, we must not speak of this without also addressing the powerful qualities which dwell within us.

The realization and use of these inner-characteristics will enable us to better handle our issues and help us to impact our surroundings.

As a believer, you need to accept the fact you are not an ordinary person. You were born with a purpose in mind.

"SET APART"

Our destiny is what God has—in advance—designated or dedicated us to do. It is what He has directed or set apart as our specific purpose or goal in life; what He has determined to be the course of the events in our human existence.

Each of us has a mission to be fulfilled, and God has equipped us to accomplish it. We should never feel inadequate or that we cannot achieve our objectives, because God has already implanted the ability within us. Remember, our challenges still come as we are walking in the will of God. We have been predestined to fulfill our destinies, and we will, even if at times it seems impossible.

A DIVINE BLUEPRINT

Prior to the time we were born, God already saw us. The Almighty declares, *"Before I formed thee in the belly I knew thee; and before thou camest forth out of the womb I sanctified thee, and I ordained thee a prophet unto the nations"* (Jeremiah 1:5).

He had total and complete knowledge of you and me. Even more, we were conceived within the being of God before He shaped us. He also knew the man and woman He would use to produce each of us.

God sees every detail of His Kingdom and His eternal plan—and the number and type of people He will need to carry it out.

We are who we are, not by our own conception, but by God's design. Our destinies were determined based upon His knowledge of us. It is clear the Father made us for His own purposes. As a result, when we walk in His predetermined path, we can accomplish what we would not have been able to do otherwise.

UNLIMITED POSSIBILITIES

Potential is the ingredient within us which can be developed and become a reality. It is what we are capable of achieving. God told Jeremiah that before he came out of the womb, He sanctified and ordained him to be a prophet. He set Jeremiah apart because He had placed within him the *potential* to be a prophet.

Remember: God does not set us apart to do a task without giving us the ability to achieve the results.

Far too many people do not succeed because they fail to operate at the level of their possibilities, but the blessings are bountiful for those who do. Here are four specific benefits:

1. They are able to conduct their lives according to divine intention.

The potential God places in each of His children will enable us to function at His desired level, and in His desired way. The Holy Spirit empowers us to discover our potential and then to live up to the standard. Our future is more easily realized when we operate in activities which He preordains. Some do not live up to their promise because they dwell in life arenas separate from God's plan. It is imperative we function in callings and activities the Lord has given us the tools to achieve in a quality manner.

2. They can operate at their highest level of ability.

If the potential to play an instrument does not lie within me, I will never play because I do not have the ability. I could practice every day and still not become accomplished. On the other hand, if I possess the gift to play an instrument, it will be manifested as I rehearse. Those blessed with God-given talent in a particular area will generally speed the progress toward excellence.

3. They can operate with power.

Great blessing comes when we function in the area of ministry God has preordained. He does not anoint the activities of some individuals because they are outside of what He has destined. When we are in His predetermined place, we will not only operate with the sharpest ability, but also with power. The Lord will significantly strengthen those who are in accordance with His Kingdom plan.

4. They can promote the work of God's Kingdom.

The plans of the Lord are always promoted when we function according to divine intention, perform at the peak level of our ability, and with His power. I am encouraging everyone who reads this book to realize God has placed within you the "Do It" factor. Whatever good thing "it" represents to you, take the great leap forward. What God has placed inwardly will help you to achieve, not only in a specific area or calling, but also in many other avenues of life. To say "I cannot do" is to promote self rejection. We can create our own downfall through negative sensory experiences such as the following:

- Negative self-talk.
- Negative self-picturing.
- Negative self-feelings (being scared, sad, angry).
- Negative self-behavior.

On the other hand, persons with high self-esteem use these sensory experiences in a positive manner. Their self-talk is uplifting; their self-picturing is realistic and favorable; their self-feelings are honorable and are properly expressed; and their self-behavior is constructive, not destructive.

The knowledge of our potential is a constant reminder of what we can do, and it is also an abiding resistance to self-rejection. It is vital to get busy working in the areas of life which significantly utilize the skills and abilities you know you possess. Through serious involvement we start to rise to the level of our potential.

HE DIRECTS OUR STEPS

Guidance from above is essential if we are going to achieve. As the psalmist writes, *"The steps of a good man are ordered by the Lord: and he delighteth in his way"* (Psalm 37:23).

A closer look at this truth produces some valuable insights:

First, He *purposes* our steps.

They reflect His divine intention. By them, His desire for our lives is manifested. God alone knows the extent of what He has placed within us. As He directs, we will walk in a manner which will enable us to realize His vision for our future.

Second, He *plans* our steps.

The Lord arranges them in a way that produces achievement. His plan includes all He intends for us—and all who will oppose us. Adherence to the leading of the Holy Spirit is essential to remain in His will and for us to overcome prevailing opposition.

Third, He *prepares* our steps.

God determines and clears the path beforehand. We succeed because He works out the details ahead of time. This preparation by Him assures that His purpose will be fulfilled—and since we follow His direction, we will not fail.

Fourth, He *provides* for our steps.

He makes provision for everything necessary for us to be successful. He will not direct us to take steps for which He has not already planned. When we rise up to achieve, He will furnish all we need for its accomplishment. God's provision is guaranteed.

Fifth, He *protects* our steps.

As we are directed or ordered by Him, no enemy or force of opposition will be victorious in their attempts to overthrow us. *"Our*

13

soul waiteth for the Lord: he is our help and our shield" (Psalm 33:2).
*"For in the time of trouble he shall hide me in his pavilion: in the
secret of his tabernacle shall he hide me: he shall set me up upon a
rock"* (Psalm 27:5).

A POSITIVE IMPACT

It is the desire of the Lord for His people to make a profound
difference in the world. This is seen in Matthew 5:13 when Jesus said
His believers are the salt of the earth. Also in Matthew 5:16, He
declares that believers are the light of the world. The Word further
states in 2 Corinthians 3:2 we are living epistles.

It is clear we have been placed on the earth to make a positive
impact. We make a difference when we are willing to let God work
through us. Then, as we commit our lives to Him and die to self, He
can operate through us more significantly. What He desires can never
be achieved without our submission to His will. Only then will we see
miraculous change.

THE PROBLEMS WE FACE

Sadly, the world is in a steady decline. A study by Planned
Parenthood revealed the following: 1. Sixty-five thousand sexual
references a year are broadcast on television. 2. The average
American television viewer now sees nearly 14,000 instances of
sexual material per year.

The Office of Applied Statistics reported that in 2001 an estimated
15.9 million Americans aged 12 or older were current illicit drug users.
Also, the percentage of the population using illicit drugs increased
from 6.3 percent in 1999 and 2000 to 7.1 percent in 2001. According
to the 1999 National Household Survey On Drug Abuse, an estimated
833,000 youths between the ages of 12-17 had carried a hand gun in
the previous year.

In our society many are addicted to drugs, sex, or alcohol. Others
are homeless. Children are abused and molested. Babies are
continually aborted and crime is prevalent.

In spite of all of this and more, we will still overcome—and our achievements will be a positive influence and a source of blessing to us and others.

THE LESSON OF NEHEMIAH

The book of Nehemiah records the restoration of Jerusalem under the leadership of the man for whom the book is named. In the biblical account, the returning Jews had a somewhat hardened indifference to God. This problem seemed to have continued because the book of Malachi denounces the Israelites for the same things.

Nehmeiah records a crucial time in Jewish history. It deals with the years after the return of God's people to their homeland around 538 B.C. This is the period following their seventy years of captivity in Babylon and Persia. At first the people were excited about rebuilding their lives and restoring the city, but the work was tiring and conditions were poor. Also, their enemies fought against them. These desperate days motivated Nehemiah to return to Jerusalem to encourage his countrymen.

THE MAN

The reason I want you to look at Nehemiah is because he faced a monumental challenge and overcame. It provides an excellent example of how to deal with opposition and still achieve success.

Nehemiah was a descendant of the Jewish population which had been taken captive to Babylon. His name means "The Lord is Consolation." He was obviously a gifted leader because it would take a determined, godly man such as he to motivate the people to act upon God's promises and rebuild the walls of Jerusalem.

We will examine the traits in his character which enabled him to fulfill his destiny. He had the privilege of being in the palace because he was the king's cupbearer, and we have no reason to believe his position caused him to compromise.

THE CALL

Nemehiah was called by the Lord for the upcoming task. Before the foundation of the world was laid, the Lord designated him for

15

leadership in this project.

Each of us has a call upon our lives. It is what the Lord has appointed and equipped us to do and is our spiritual vocation or profession. In the natural, we attend colleges and universities to study for work in our chosen fields. In the spiritual, realm we dedicate ourselves to God to carry out the mission He has chosen for us. He determines our callings.

Our God-given purpose and what we desire to achieve are accompanied by burden, which plays a significant role in our achievement.

Nehemiah inquired with Hanani and other brethren concerning the Jews who were in Jerusalem. They told Nehemiah the people were in great affliction, the wall of Jerusalem was crumbling and the city gates were burned by fire. Nehemiah had questions for them because he had a burden to aid in the restoration of his people and his homeland. After receiving the tragic news, he sat down and wept. He also fasted, prayed and mourned for many days and his response manifested his yearning to accept the task before him.

The burden to achieve is vitally important for the following reasons:

1. It identifies us with persons affected by our calling.

- A burden for the homeless identifies us with the homeless.
- A burden for addicts identifies us with addicts.
- A burden for abused children identifies us with abused children.
- A burden for prisoners identifies us with those who are incarcerated.
- A burden for foreign missions identifies us with those of other nations.

2. It motivates us to do what we are called to do. It can affect our appetite, our sleep, our rest, and our peace of mind.

3. It is a reminder of where we are to focus our attention.

4. It keeps us striving to improve ourselves and the conditions in the areas of our callings.

5. It drives us to overcome hurdles which block our achievement.

6. It promotes the increase of our commitment.

7. It fosters consistency.

8. It resists stagnation and laziness.

9. It will drive us to do, even if no one else does.

10. It will cause us to commit all of our resources to achieve.

11. It will empower us to work long hours for success.

Like Nehemiah, we must respond to the burden. In essence, this is proof it has been received.

So often I have talked with individuals who desperately wanted their situations to change, yet they were not driven by a passion for transformation and their circumstances did not improve. Nehemiah sat down and wept because the heavy burden caused him to identify with his people. He grieved and was sorrowful.

He understood the importance of prayer and, as a result of petitioning God, he conquered. This is essential when we have a mission to accomplish. Through prayer:

- We can maintain our worship of the Lord.
- We can make our concerns known to God.
- We receive direction from the Father.
- We receive heavenly power in earthly activities.
- We receive perpetual power.
- We experience intimacy with God.

- The energies of The Almighty are released to us.
- We can ask the Lord to do what we cannot.
- We can be empowered to achieve the challenges before us.

After we realize the burden, we must respond accordingly, then God will intervene on our behalf.

THE NEHEMIAH CHARACTER

When you combine all the traits that make us who we are, it's called *character*. They can be good or bad, yet *we* are as *they* are. Our character is developed as a result of a process. It is not created all at once, but is painfully and laboriously built over time.

Habits of love, hate, falsehood, truth, righteousness or goodness all silently shape our characters until it garments us with the likeness of God. Whatever the Father calls us to do, He gives us the ability to develop the required character necessary. He has placed within each of us the ability to face and overcome every circumstance, even the current one which seems to have us defeated. Let me assure you from personal experience, regardless how bleak the situation looks, you can overcome.

Why did Nehemiah succeed?

First: Nehemiah was *consecrated* to God.

He was sacred and set apart to the Lord. The sense of scripture is that he was serious in his relationship with the Father. His immediate response on hearing the bad news concerning his countrymen was to fast and pray. He prayed always, not only just when trouble arose. God called him for the assignment and had placed in him the ability to be a consecrated vessel, taking on the character of God.

Second: Nehemiah was *committed* to God.

He had been equipped by the Lord to become a committed vessel. He had brought himself under subjection and assigned himself to do God's will. *"Commit thy way unto the Lord; trust also in him; and he shall bring it to pass"* (Psalm 37:5). He willingly responded to the charge given him by the Lord and was loyal and dependable. He was committed to his people and the "cause" that would restore them.

Third: Nehemiah was *consistent* with God.

His service to the Lord was without negative variation. He operated at a quality level and he did so with regularity.

Fouth: Nehemiah was *constant* with God.

He was steadfast and unmovable. *"Therefore my beloved brethren, be ye steadfast, unmovable, always abounding in the work of the Lord, forasmuch as ye know that your labour is not in vain in the Lord"* (1 Corinthians 15:58).

THE FAITH FACTOR

Nehemiah was a man of tremendous faith who believed and trusted God. Here's what unshakable faith does:

1. It enables us to trust God when it seems the end has come.
2. It enables us to step out to fulfill our call rather than procrastinate.
3. It enables us to see our work fulfilled before it is completed.
4. It enables us to see victories, even while we are still battling.
5. It enables us to view opposition as opportunity.
6. It enables us to take the first step, even if we don't know how we will take the second.
7. It enables us to work, knowing God will provide for what He has called us to do.
8. It enables us to maintain the actions necessary to please God in our callings.
9. It enables us to achieve that which was previously impossible.
10. It enables us to keep hope alive in the midst of affliction.
11. It enables us to dance and rejoice when our situations say we should cry.

OUR WORK ETHIC

Nehemiah was a dedicated worker. He served faithfully and in a quality manner as the king's cupbearer—performing so well that the king had a genuine appreciation for him. So many people possess the ability to overcome obstacles, but fail simply because they have poor work habits. The Bible tells us, *"The hand of the diligent shall bear rule: but the slothful shall be under tribute"* (Proverbs 12:24). *"The soul of the sluggard desireth and hath nothing: but the soul of the diligent shall be made fat"* (Proverbs 13:4).

The word "fat" in the above verse means "anointed" or "satisfied." This is a reward for the industrious person.

THE COMMISSION OF NEHEMIAH

The Lord calls us—and after we answer the call, He *commissions* us. The word itself means to authorize or command to act in a prescribed manner, even to be an agent or representative of someone else. Nehemiah responded to God's voice and was now ready to receive the Almighty's authority to act on His behalf and go to Jerusalem.

All believers have been commissioned by the Lord to engage in Kingdom business and to defeat and overthrow the obstacles before us. When the burden upon Nehemiah grew heavy, he offered prayer to God, asking the Lord to grant him mercy in the sight of his employer, the king. He knew the time had come for him to take action in relation to his people in Jerusalem.

We too must know when it is our time to act. Too many allow their negative situations to linger and their dreams to be put on hold. They have planned for a long time, yet have not moved forward in faith. Everything is ready for implementation, but nothing is being done. Instead, they sit around and state reasons why they cannot begin.

Some wait so long they begin to doubt their calling. They offer excuses: not enough money, inadequate help, or not enough family support—inwardly building a case against themselves.

Nehemiah had both a burden and a dream; a deep yearning for his people and a vision to be instrumental in helping them. He did not procrastinate, instead he moved forward into action. The burden within Nehemiah intensified—his time had arrived.

At the palace, he served the king wine as he had always done. Through all of his experiences, he managed to maintain a positive demeanor in the king's presence. However, on this particular day the burden was visible on his countenance. When the king saw his sadness, he questioned why he looked that way, knowing he was not sick. The king recognized his servant's sorrow of heart.

Nehemiah informed the king the place of his fathers' grave was lying in waste and ruin and the gates of the city had been burned with fire. Here was a man who was ready and willing to take his commission.

GOD'S FAVOR

The Lord gave Nehemiah favor with the king. This approving regard is demonstrated by kindness beyond what is expected or deserved. Such consideration causes others to grant us privileges.

The king asked Nehemiah what he wanted to do. Nehemiah requested a leave of absence so he could travel to Jerusalem and work to rebuild the walls. The king inquired how long his journey would take and when he would return. He allowed Nehemiah to set the length of time he would be gone.

According to scripture, both the king and his wife trusted Nehemiah. Every believer should earn the confidence of their employers—which is established by quality character.

Nehemiah requested that letters be sent to the governors beyond the river so he could travel to Jerusalem without hindrance. He also asked a letter be sent to Asaph, the keeper of the forest, so he would provide lumber to make beams for the gates of the palace and the walls of the city. The Bible records the king granted Nehemiah according to the good hand of God upon him. The king also sent captains of the army and horsemen to accompany Nehemiah.

Favor is a sign of God's approval which enables us to succeed beyond our ability to achieve and even causes those who hate us to help. It makes the impossible become possible. This is why the attempt of our enemy to destroy us will fail—and why obstacles will fall before us and our dreams and visions will be fulfilled.

Scripture speaks clearly regarding our favor:

■ There is no want to us that fear Him (Psalm 34:9).

- His eyes are upon us (v.15).
- He inclines His ear to us (Psalm 40:1).
- In the time of trouble He hides us in His pavilion (Psalm 27:5).
- He surrounds us with favor (Psalm 5:12).
- He is our defense (Psalm 7:10).
- He is our salvation (Psalm 62:7).

STEPS TO CONQUERING

Before we venture out to fulfill our dreams and visions, or to win the battle, we must make certain that we are "together" ourselves. The following ten steps are essential:

One: We must achieve personal restoration.

We cannot expect to conquer or to significantly help others if we have too many personal unresolved issues. The fulfillment of our dreams require a total focused effort. We must be restored from past hurts, abuses, failures, financial devastation, divorces, separations, sinful acts, disappointment, discouragement, and more.

Through the process of our personal healing and rebuilding, we will experience an increase in our faith and gain knowledge which will enhance our ability to succeed. Also, we will be able to identify with others who have gone through the same thing.

Two: We must realize that our stepping out will grieve our enemies.

When Nehemiah left, his enemies learned of his departure. Sanballat the Horonite and Tobiah the Ammonite heard the news and it grieved them exceedingly. They were upset because Nehemiah had gone to help God's people.

As long as we are stagnant, not moving forward, our enemies will be content, but once we rise up to fulfill our dreams, they will be upset. Why? Because their grip will be broken from the lives of those who will benefit from our actions.

Here is what we can expect from our enemies:

22

1. They will seek to hinder God's work (1 Thessalonians 2:18).
2. They will seek to resist our prayers (Daniel 10:12).
3. They will seek to blind people to the truth (2 Corinthians 4:4).
4. They will lay snares for us (2 Timothy 2:26).
5. They will tempt us (Matthew 4:1).
6. They will seek to afflict us (Job 2:7).
7. They will seek to deceive us (Revelation 12:9).

Paul accurately sums it up: *"Now thanks be unto God, which always causeth us to triumph in Christ..."* Corinthians 2:14). *"Now unto Him that is able to do exceeding abundantly above all that we ask or think according to the power that worketh in us"* (Ephesians 3:20).

He makes it clear that to defeat the enemy we must, by the power *in* us, allow the Lord to do mightily *through* us. If we allow Him, He will do exceeding (over, above, beyond, superior to, more) abundantly (beyond measure, very highly) above all we ask or think. This means that He will do:

- Superior to Superior
- Beyond "Beyond Measure"
- More Than "More"
- Above "Very Highly"
- Advantage "Beyond Advantage"

Three: We must prayerfully select those who will work with us.

Communing with the Lord concerning those who will help you is essential. Nehemiah only had a few men go with him. Those who work with us should have the following attributes:

1. They should be in serious relationship with the Lord.
2. They should love God, live and labor for Him.
3. They should identify with the burden we have for those we will serve, as well as for the dreams and visions we are to realize.

4. They should be qualified, diligent workers who will not quit.
5. They should promote harmony in their relationships with others.
6. They should be currently involved in work in God's Kingdom.

Over the years of my pastorate I have watched many patiently endure, while some have grown weary or disgruntled, and others have backslidden. When we take up our commission, we must have individuals of quality character helping us.

Four: We must prayerfully determine when to share our vision.

Nehemiah did not tell anyone except the king and his wife what was in his heart. Be careful with whom you share your dream, because some may not be excited concerning what the Lord is doing in your life.

Certainly, Nehemiah did not want to stir up too much opposition before he began his mission. The Lord knows those who will work on our behalf and He will reveal them to us. He has preordained certain persons to help. He has either already prepared them or is doing so at this very moment.

God has predetermined the skills we will need and He has placed those abilities in the individuals who will assist us. The provision of labor and finances have been predetermined. Keep praying and waiting on the Lord until He brings those He has designated.

In the meantime we should be sure that we clearly understand our own obstacles, visions, and dreams. We must know what the Lord wants us to do before we can lead others in its fulfillment.

Five: We must prayerfully count the cost.

Nehemiah prayed and considered what his mission entailed before he left on this momentous assignment After he arrived in Jerusalem, he went out after three days to survey the land—wanting to see how much work they would have to do. His personal evaluation of the project was important:

- It revealed the work to be done.
- It revealed the extent of the damage.
- It revealed information which enabled him to determine the cost of repairs.
- It revealed the extent of the need for labor.
- It revealed information that enabled Nehemiah to organize the work force.

We must always take an inventory and determine the cost of every undertaking in our life. It is disappointing to put tireless effort into a project and then have to abandon it because of lack of finances or other resources. As Jesus says, *"For which of you, intending to build a tower, sitteth not down first, and counteth the cost, whether he have sufficient to finish it?"* (Luke. 14:28).

Six: We must know we have God's provision.

In Matthew 10, Jesus gave His disciples a commission, telling them to heal the sick, cleanse lepers, raise the dead and cast out devils. Then, in Matthew 6 and Luke 12, Jesus spoke to His disciples concerning *provision,* saying:

1. Take no thought for your life. He did not want them to worry concerning what they would eat or drink.

2. Take no thought for your body. He did not want them to be anxious over their clothing.

3. Consider the ravens. He said they neither see nor reap. They have neither storehouses or barns, but God feeds them. He asks, are you better than the fowls?

4. Which of you can add one cubit to your stature by thinking about it? Worrying over provision does not produce results. We are not to be anxious, rather to trust God. If we cannot do the small things, why should we worry over larger problems? The word "cubit" literally means "measure of space or distance" (approximately eighteen inches). It can also mean a measure of time or age (John 9:21). So the verse can read either "who can add one cubit to his stature" or "one minute to his life span."

5. Consider the lilies. They do not toil for money to buy clothing

25

JEROME STOKES

or spin cloth to make what they wear. Yet they are more beautifully arrayed than Solomon in all his glory. If God so clothed the lilies which today "are" and tomorrow "are not," how much more will He clothe us. He says, "O ye of little faith."

The Lord instructed them not to seek what they would eat or drink. Additionally, He told them they shouldn't be of a doubtful mind because of negativity:

- It causes us to distrust rather than to trust God.
- It causes us to hesitate when we should take action.
- It causes us to worry over provision rather than rely on the Lord.
- It causes us to miss blessings we should have possessed.

Jesus told the people in His day, and He speaks to us, saying the Father knows we have need of these things. If we seek the Kingdom of God and His righteousness, they will be provided to us.

Seven: We must properly share the vision with those who will help us.

The vision is God's, not ours. After Nehemiah surveyed the work to be done, he shared the dream with others.

It is important to know what you are striving to achieve. Nehemiah told those around him of the hand of God resting upon his life. He also shared the words the king had spoken—and what he had done on his behalf. As a result, they knew the Lord was with Nehemiah.

This man of God understood that the cause he was striving for was the Almighty's cause. His work was for his nation, not for personal gain, but it would require the Lord's help and the assistance of others. Nehemiah had to explain his vision to the people before they would work with him for its achievement.

The more individuals we have who clearly understand the dream, and who seriously identify with it, the greater the effort will be to achieve success. After he shared the vision they said, "Let us rise up and build."

Repeatedly we will need others to help us. This is true for

26

mastering personal struggles, starting and operating ministries or businesses, overcoming family hardships, and more.

Eight: We must develop a strategy to achieve.

When challenges arise, we must not be so fearful and preoccupied with them that we fail to develop strategies and plans. Sitting around worrying will not bring about victory.

Nehemiah surveyed the city so he could see what needed to be done. This enabled him to develop a plan of action for the restoration process.

There were twelve gates of Jerusalem which had fallen into disrepair:

1. Sheep Gate (Nehemiah 3:1). The sheep for sacrifice were brought through this gate.
2. Fish Gate (v.3). Fish from the Jordan and the Sea of Galilee were brought through this entrance.
3. Old Gate (v.6). Believed to be the main gate.
4. Valley Gate (v.13).
5. Dung Gate (v.14). Refuse was carried out through this gate to the general garbage disposal site.
6. Fountain Gate (v.15).
7. Water Gate (v.26).
8. Horse Gate (v.28). It was so named because of the many horses connected with the kings of Israel.
9. East Gate (v.29). It was east of the temple and connected to its structure.
10. Miphrad Gate (v.31).
11. Ephraim Gate (Nehemiah 8:16).
12. Prison Gate (Nehemiah 3:25).

Nehemiah developed a blueprint for achievement. For example, he assigned the High Priests as the leaders in rebuilding the Sheep gate and specific leaders and families to restore each of the other entrances. He organized the work so it could be completed in an orderly fashion. His planning and preparation was the result of his daily communion with the Lord. A further look at his strategy reveals the following:

- They prayed to God and set a watch day and night (Nehemiah 4:9).
- They only took off their clothes to wash because they had guard duty (v.23).
- They planned to gather with Nehemiah if they heard the sound of the trumpet (v.20).
- They worked with a tool in one hand and a weapon in the other (v.17).
- They set families with their swords, spears, and bows behind the wall (v.13).

The plan provided an organized approach as well as promoted the unity of the workers.

Nine: We must know that we will prosper.

When Israel's enemies, Sanballat and Tobiah, heard of the intention to build, they laughed them to scorn. They accused Nehemiah and Israel of rebelling against the king. Nehemiah responded, *"The God of heaven, he will prosper us; therefore we his servants will arise and build..."* (Nehemiah 2:20). He was unwavering in his belief that God would bless them.

When we step out to do works for the Lord, fulfill our dreams or to overcome problems in our lives, we must do so in His confidence, knowing we will succeed. Psalm 1 says when we walk with the Lord, "whatsoever we do will prosper." We must declare our abundance by claiming:

1. "I will go in the strength of the Lord God" (Psalm 71:16).
2. "I am a wonder unto many but, God is my strong refuge" (v.8).
3. "God will increase my greatness, and comfort me on every side" (v.21).
4. "In God have I put my trust" (Psalm 56:11).
5. "The Lord upholdeth me with His right hand" (Psalm 37:24).
6. "The arms of the wicked shall be broken" (v.17).

7. "I am righteous and will never be forsaken by the Lord" (v.25).

If we boldly face our challenges with undaunted faith, we will prosper and be effective. Go with a determination that the obstacles will be met and defeated.

When Sanballat and Tobiah heard of the progress of Nehemiah and the others, they became bitterly angry and mocked, saying, "What are these feeble Jews doing? Will they fortify themselves? Will they sacrifice? Will they revive the stones out of the heaps of rubbish which are burned?"

In spite of all the negative chatter of the enemy, Nehemiah stood his ground, firm in the belief he and Israel would prosper.

We must be so assured of victory that nothing said or done can change our mindset. Our faith is proven when we can be rock-solid in our "conquering expectation," regardless of the discouragement we encounter.

God needs believers who will live with a determination to overcome all opposition—and be used by the Lord to change environments, cities, nations and the world. Tobiah chided them, saying, the wall they were building would break down even if a fox climbed on it. Yet, Nehemiah and the people persisted and were effective.

Ten: We must have a mind to conquer.

Nehemiah indicates they completed the rebuilding project because the people had a passion to work. A "made up mind" is essential because it is a settled, resolved, concluded one. It is also an expression of our love for the Lord because it says to Him that of all the choices we have, we chose Him as He chose us. It says we will forsake all for Him, and endure hardship because we give God the priority in our lives.

I have found that a genuine love for the Lord, properly embedded within us, produces a mind which will not allow failure. It tells us not to settle for less, but to strive for the best, and that the obstacles in front of us will be moved. It is a mind which is both made up for Christ and against the enemy.

Sanballat sent word to Nehemiah saying he wanted to talk to him. Nehemiah responded, "I am doing a great work, so that I cannot come down: why should the work cease, whilst I leave it, and come down to you?"

He had a determination to fulfill God's work and refused to be distracted. Neither should we. Though Israel had subsequent problems, Nehemiah led them to conquer every force of opposition they encountered, and they faithfully completed the task.

CHAPTER 2

YOU ARE A KINGDOM CONQUEROR

In church services we often speak of the fact "we are more than conquerors." It is an uplifting and encouraging promise from God's Word.

Faced with the challenges of life, we need to be reminded of who we are in Christ—and a study of the believer's walk brings understanding of *why* we are more than conquerors.

What we are discussing is far greater than simply defeating enemies. We can triumph to the extent we make footstools out of our foes, and launching pads out of our roadblocks!

Why is it necessary for us to learn to be conquerors?

- We will experience tribulation.
  "...in the world ye shall have tribulation" (John 16:33).
- We will experience fiery trials.
  "Beloved think it not strange concerning the fiery trial which is to try you, as though some strange thing happened unto you" (1 Peter 4:12).
- We will experience heavy attack.
  "I am troubled; I am bowed down greatly; I go mourning all the day long" (Psalm 38:6).
- We will experience pits.
  "He brought me up also out of an horrible pit, out of the miry clay and set my feet upon a rock, and established my goings" (Psalm 40:2).
- We will experience abundance and better days.
  Jesus declares, *"...I am come that they might have life, and that*

they might have it more abundantly" (John 10:10).

However, on the path to becoming a conqueror, there are three important factors we must know:

First: We should consider our past condition.

We were born into a state of separation from the Almighty due to the fall of Adam. Mankind died spiritually, and this death means severance from the sustaining presence of God. We were out of fellowship with the Father and were not fit to enjoy heavenly things.

The spiritually dead are neither charmed or alarmed by spiritual things. We were dead in sin and separated from Christ—and without Him our lives were without hope in this life and in the life to come. It was a condition of bondage. We were bound by sin and under its control, following its dictates.

Second: We must consider the Precious Gift.

Among the things Isaiah said concerning Jesus is that His name shall be called Wonderful (Isaiah 9:6). In God's Son we see:

- *A wonderful exhibition.* The life and benefit of Christ is a demonstration of the grace of God. Through Jesus the attributes of God flowed out to save us. He was an exposition, a living sermon of the goodness of God. This was seen at Calvary in Jesus' love, suffering and death for guilty humanity.
- *A wonderful character.* Jesus is the Great God and Savior (Titus 2:13). He manifested the character of the Father in the earth, the only *perfected* character.
- *A wonderful gift.* The work of Christ was to redeem and cleanse. When one purchases a fine set of silverware, it is not used until it is cleansed. It is purchased and then washed. The Lord uses us, not because we are worthy or gifted, but because we are made clean. He has begun a good work in us and will continue to perform it.
- *A wonderful people.* As the redeemed and purified of the

Lord, we are God's peculiar people—blessed to be conformed to the image and likeness of Christ. We are the salt of the earth and the light of the world.

- *A wonderful life.* It is an existence which reflects back on a dark world, the image of the invisible God. It is also a life beaming with the gentleness and truthfulness of Jesus and His abundance.
- *A wonderful prospect.* We are looking for His glorious appearing. May we be prepared for this marvelous day.

Third: We must consider our present condition.

We have been saved by grace and are seated with Christ in heavenly places. This gives us access to the Father and we are fellow-citizens of heaven. Thank God, we are joint heirs with Christ.

OUR UNIQUE POSITION

Jesus has made great provision for us to enjoy. The fact we are in a special place in Christ means we are unique. Let's look at what our position says about us.

1. We are a chosen people.

Scripture declares: *"For thou art an holy people unto the Lord thy God, and the Lord hath chosen thee to be a peculiar people unto Himself, above all the nations that are upon the earth"* (Deuteronomy 14:2). *"But ye are a chosen generation, a royal priesthood, an holy nation, a peculiar people; that ye should show forth the praises of Him who hath called you out of darkness into His marvelous light"* (1 Peter 2:9).

In the infinite wisdom and knowledge of God, He chose us:

- With our family lineages and backgrounds.
- With our shortcomings and limitations.
- With our education—or lack of.
- With our large and small salaries.
- With our successes and failures.

- With our races, creeds and nationalities.
- With our wealth or poverty.

He chose us to be a new race of people; a species which is different from all others.

2. We are a royal people.

In the above scripture (1 Peter 2:9) we are referred to as the "royal priesthood." It's true. We are priests of royalty who belong to the Sovereign King of the Universe. We live, move and have our being in Him.

- We have the *power* of the King, the power over self, the world system and Satan.
- We have the *riches* of the King, the unsearchable riches of Christ.
- We have the *apparel* of the King, the robe of Christ.
- We have the *face* of the King, and sit at His table taking in the royal diet of the Word of God.
- We have the *retinue* of the King, having angels to serve and guard us.

3. We are the apple of His eye.

The psalmist prayed, *"Keep me as the apple of the eye, hide me under the shadow of thy wings"* (Psalm 17:8).
Because of this:

- He upholds our goings in His path (Psalm 17:5).
- He inclines His ear to us (v.6).
- He shows us His marvelous loving kindness (v.7).
- He saves us by His right hand (v.7).
- He hides us under the shadow of His wings (v.8).
- He encloses the wicked who oppress us, in their own fat (v.10).
- He rains snares, fire and brimstone upon the wicked (Psalm 11:6).

- He arises for us and disappoints our enemies (Psalm 17:13).

4. We are in relationship with Him.

Our bond of fellowship with Christ is unquestionably a major reason we conquer.

He is the Head, we are the body. *"And he is the head of the body, the church..."* (Colossians 1:18). As His body, we are under His guidance and control. Our lives are not our own; they belong to Him. We think like Him, love like Him, live like Him, and give like Him. We are in subjection to the Lord and are united together.

He is the Vine, we are the branches. Jesus declares, *"I am the vine, ye are the branches..."* (John 15:5). He is the source of the very life we experience. His power is the strength we operate by; therefore, we meet and conquer every challenge. As long as we are connected, all of our needs will be met and He enables us to bring forth much fruit.

He is the Shepherd, we are the sheep. *"I am the good shepherd: the good shepherd giveth his life for the sheep"* (John 10:11).

- Jesus is the Good Shepherd (John 10:11). He is called "good" because He risked and sacrificed His life for the sheep.
- Jesus is the Great Shepherd (Hebrews 13:20-21). He is called "great" because He arose from the dead and He perfects the sheep.
- Jesus is Shepherd and Bishop of our souls (1 Peter 2:25). He is called the "Shepherd" because He invites those who went astray.
- Jesus is the Chief Shepherd (1. Peter 5:4) As such, He cares and provides for us.

Our relationship with Him connects us with His omnipotence.

God is all-powerful and can do anything if it does not contradict His own nature. He has power over the universe, separates light from darkness (Genesis 1:14), divides the firmament (v.7), separates seas from dry land (v.10) and weighs mountains in His scale (Isaiah 40:12). He has authority over men, angels, Satan, demons, and death. Even more, our relationship with Him provides access to this power. With the Lord, whatever we encounter we can handle.

Our relationship with Him calls us to His omniscience.

The Almighty is all-knowing. He possesses, without prior discovery, complete and universal knowledge of all things past, present, and future. This not only includes the actual, but also the *possible* which may never become real. He has total and immediate knowledge of all things. Whatever we encounter, He understands it fully. He knows our challenges, dreams and the tactics, traps and devices of the enemy.

Our relationship with Him convinces us of His omnipresence.

God, in the totality of His essence, without diffusion or expansion, multiplication or division, penetrates and fills the universe in all its parts. He is everywhere present. This speaks of His being in the world, acting within and through His creation. His transcendence affirms that God is above and beyond all. Whenever we need Him, He is always present to enable us to conquer.

Our relationship with Him provides us with access to all of His divine attributes. With such empowerment, how can we fail?

5. We are heavenly citizens.

In an earthly sense, we are citizens of the city and nation where we live—and we owe our allegiance to the government over us. However, when we came to Christ we became new creatures, and also received *heavenly* citizenship. In Ephesians 2, Paul says we are no more strangers and foreigners, but fellow citizens with the saints, and of the household of God. This is acquired by birth and we are born into our Father's family.

The natural law provides citizenship to a child because of the blood relationship with his or her parents. However, heavenly citizenship does not come through natural parentage, but by our relationship with Christ through His shed blood. The natural law also provides citizenship to persons born within a country's borders. Our spiritual birth takes place within the boundaries of God's Kingdom.

Our citizenship requires education. Foreigners must come through the Americanization Program to prepare them for being a legal resident. They must understand U.S. history, government structure, policies and other requirements. Believers must engage in what I call the "Heavenization" Program. They must learn the requirements of heavenly citizens and study our citizenship manual, The Bible. They must know about God, godly living, praise, worship, spiritual warfare and more. Our heavenly citizenship entitles us to all of the promises of God in the scriptures.

Also, it does not expire with this life—it is eternal. When we go to be with the Lord, our heavenly citizenship will still be in effect.

There are great benefits involved. We are now pilgrims in the earth, journeying through it. Yes, we are strangers, sojourners, and temporary residents, yet there are privileges:

- We have been raised up and made to sit in heavenly places (Ephesians 2:6).
- We have been made near to God by the blood of Jesus Christ (v.13).
- We are founded upon Christ (v.20).
- We are built together for an habitation of God through the Spirit (v.22).
- We have boldness and access with confidence by faith (Ephesians 3:12).
- We have been granted according to the riches of His glory to be strengthened with might by His Spirit in the inner man (v.16).
- We are no longer tossed to and fro with every wind of doctrine (Ephesians.4:14).

Yes, we reside here on earth, but our citizenship is in Heaven.

6. We have open doors before us.

The work of Jesus was the work of a divine Opener. Sin had closed the door into every spiritual privilege, but Jesus now holds the keys of death and Hell.

There is an open door of deliverance. God's Son tells us, *"I am the door: by me if any man enter, he shall be saved..."* (John 10:9). When we entered into Christ, we escaped the wrath of God. In an on-going way we experience the salvation of the Lord. He delivers us continually from sin, danger, demonic attacks, enemy traps, generational curses, mental scars from abuse, and old habits which grip us.

There is an open door of direction. We are privileged because we are taught by the Lord. If we desire wisdom, we can ask. The door into the divine chamber is now open through Christ. The Lord presents the scriptures to us and anoints our minds to receive revelation of the wonderful things in His Word. *"Hear counsel and receive instruction, that thou mayest be wise in thy latter end"* (Proverbs 19:20).

We are directed through heavenly instruction which produces the best life and positions us for achievement. It protects us from unnecessary hardship and promotes the fulfillment of our purpose. It also provides wisdom to properly conduct our lives and enables us to endure difficulty. This guidance prepares us for Kingdom assignments and assures the completion of them.

There is an open door of discourse. We win great victories through prayer—our communion with the Lord. Nothing lies beyond its reach except that which is outside of the will of God. Prayer moves the arm that moves the world.

- Moses prayed and a nation was saved.
- Joshua prayed and the sun stood still as the enemy was defeated.
- Hannah prayed and God gave her a son.
- Solomon prayed for wisdom and became the wisest of mortal men.

- Elijah prayed and God sent rain and fire.
- Jonah prayed and was released from the whale.
- Three Hebrews prayed and were delivered from a fiery furnace.
- Elisha prayed and received a double portion of Elijah's spirit.
- Daniel prayed and was not harmed while in a den of lions.
- Peter prayed and Dorcas arose from the dead.
- The disciples prayed and the Holy Spirit came.

We are kingdom conquerors because we pray.

There is an open door of duty.

As children of God, we are to work in His kingdom. Christ does not compel us to serve or to follow Him, rather He commands and invites.

When we serve in various ministries in the church, we will change for the better. Serving resists slothfulness and complacency. It promotes growth and development, reveals leadership skills and teaches us to best relate to others. It can promote prayer and fasting and deepen our commitment to the Lord. Service to God enables us to gain spiritual warfare skills that will help us to overcome enemy attacks.

There is an open door of dunamis.

The power (dunamis) of God is given to help us do a spiritual thing in a spiritual way in an unspiritual world. This power is not social, monetary, intellectual, political, military or physical. It is the power of Almighty God.

7. We possess abiding joy.

What is joy? It is inner gladness, deep rooted pleasure, depth of assurance and confidence which ignites a cheerful heart. True joy is possessed and given only by God. Its roots are not in earthly or material objects and does not depend on circumstances.

Some Christians may have sad faces, but every true believer in God has a joyful heart. Even if our lives seem overwhelmed with trouble, they are also full of joy. For us, adversity is temporary, but joy is eternal. Why? Because our joy is from the Lord and the quality of it can only be provided by Him. It resembles the calm of the settled water in the deep sea, undisturbed by those elements which constantly affect the surface.

Our joy is in the Lord. *"Yet will I rejoice in the Lord, I will joy in the God of my salvation"* (Habakkuk 3:18). This implies knowledge of God because we cannot rejoice in the Lord unless we know Him.

This joy is a celebration and an expression of who He is and all that He does. We rejoice in Him because He is who He is.

Since we look for and expect the best, our joy is one of anticipation. Our lives are not only full of happiness, but also full of progress. We are constantly climbing from one high place of grace to another. We do not grab at bubbles which evaporate, but we lay hold on spiritual certainties.

Our expectation is strong because the feet of our faith rest on and cling to the amazing and precious promises of God. We stand in anticipation:

- That the Lord is soon to return.
- That we will stand fast in our liberty in Christ.
- That we will overcome every attack against us.
- That we will fulfill our purposes in Christ.
- That the peace of God will rule in our hearts.
- That we will serve the Lord in quality fellowship with other believers.
- That we will be mightily used by Him.
- That lost souls will be drawn to Christ in increasing numbers.

Our joy is independent of earthly activities. We rejoice in the face of all types of circumstances, because we look at the outward through the eyes of our inward happiness.

By the power of the Holy Spirit, we focus on what we know God will do, as opposed to what we are going through. It is clear to us that we will experience both difficult and easy times, yet we are counseled, "Rejoice in the Lord always: and again I say, Rejoice" (Philippians 4:4).

One reason we are more than conquerors is because we have joy in the furnace of affliction, in the pits of life, during times of lack, and in times of betrayal.

THE ULTIMATE CONQUEROR

The best example of a Victor is Jesus Christ. His life is representative of the way we are to conduct ourselves:

Who was Jesus?

"Was" is not used in the sense that He no longer exists, but to make reference to the time when He walked the earth.

He was the Mighty God.

"For unto us a child is born, unto us a son is given: and the government shall be upon his shoulder: and his name shall be called Wonderful, Counselor, The Mighty God, The Everlasting Father, the Prince of Peace" (Isaiah 9:6).

He was God with us.

"Therefore the Lord himself shall give you a sign; Behold a virgin shall conceive, and bear a son, and shall call his name Immanuel" (Isaiah 7:14). Matthew 1:23 interprets Emmanuel to mean, "God with us."

He was God in the flesh.

"And without controversy great is the mystery of godliness: God was manifest in the flesh, justified in the Spirit, seen of angels, preached unto the Gentiles, believed on in the world, received up into glory" (1 Timothy 3:16).

He was the Son of God.

"...for that which is conceived in her is of the Holy Ghost" (Matthew 1:20).

41

Where did Jesus come from?

He came from heaven.

In John 8:42, Jesus says He proceeded and came from God. Referring to Jesus, the Bible declares, *"And no man hath ascended up to heaven, but he that came down from heaven, even the Son of man which is in heaven"* (John 3:13).

How did Jesus come?

- He took on flesh (1 Timothy 3:16).
- He was born of a virgin (Matthew 1:18-25).
- He came as a servant (Philippians 2:7).
- He came in a lowly manner (Matthew 11:29).

Why did Jesus come?

- To save the lost (Luke 19:10).
- To die for us (Romans 8:5).
- To reveal the invisible God (John 1:14).
- To fulfill prophecy (Matthew 5:17-18).
- To reconcile man to God (2 Corinthians 5:19).
- To be our perfect example (1 Peter 2:21).
- To destroy the works of the devil (Hebrew 2:14).
- To be our High Priest (v.17).
- To preach, heal, and liberate (Luke 4:18-19).

OVERCOMING TEMPTATION

In Matthew 4:1-11, Jesus was about to launch His ministry —which would affect the lives of all who would ever live. To be prepared spiritually, mentally and physically; He spent time alone with the Father, and He fasted forty days and forty nights.

Once He received the strength to go forward, there was one factor missing in His preparation. Jesus had to be confronted by the temptations He would face in the near future. That's when He was led by the Spirit into the wilderness.

The first temptation.

The Son of God was asked to use His power for personal reasons. Satan said to Jesus, "If thou be the Son of God, command that these stones be made bread."

Jesus responded, "It is written, Man shall not live by bread alone, but by every word that proceedeth out of the mouth of God." The enemy tempts us in our areas of need during our wilderness experiences, trying to appeal to the lust of the flesh.

The second temptation.

Jesus was tempted to prove His deity by the spectacular. Satan told Jesus that if He was the Son of God, to cast Himself down from the pinnacle, for God would protect Him. The Lord told the devil, "It is written, Thou shalt not tempt the Lord thy God."

Satan appeals to the pride of life.

The third temptation.

Jesus was tempted to compromise. Satan showed Him all the kingdoms of the world, and the glory of them. He said he would give it all to Jesus if He fell down and worshiped him. Jesus boldly responded, "Get thee hence, Satan: for it is written, Thou shalt worship the Lord thy God, and him only shalt thou serve."

Satan can entice us when we look at all that is available in the world to attract the flesh. This temptation appeals to the lust of the eyes.

Jesus overcame the greatest temptations Satan could offer—and in the process, conquered him.

AUTHORITY OVER DEMONS

Demons are spiritual beings which are corrupt and hostile to both God and man. They are fallen angels, deathless creatures that serve Satan. The level and intensity of demonic activity in people during the time of Christ's ministry was high because of His attacks on Satan's kingdom. But Jesus cast out demons in large numbers during His earthly ministry.

Demons serve as the hands and feet of Satan. They cause the mental state of some to be unbalanced and can control a person's actions, thoughts and deeds. Jesus cast out demons that caused convulsions (Luke. 4:35), insanity (Matthew 8:32), speechlessness (Matthew 9:33), blindness (Matthew12:22) and paralysis (Luke. 13:10-17).

Every believer needs to be aware that any demonic power we encounter, including Satan, has already been defeated by Jesus. As Kingdom conquerors, we will walk and face these forces in a manner which reflects our knowledge they have been overcome by Jesus.

AUTHORITY OVER PHYSICAL CONDITIONS
Everywhere Jesus journeyed, there were miracles of healing:

- A leper (Matthew 8:1).
- A paralytic (Matthew 9:1).
- A woman with an issue of blood (v.20).
- Two blind men (vv.27-31).
- A man with a withered hand (Matthew 12:10).
- A severed ear (Matthew 26:51).
- A deaf man with a speech problem (Mark 7:31).
- A nobleman's son (John 4:50).
- A crippled man (John 5:1-16).

Jesus was the Greater Force against every resistant force. Whenever the Greater meets the lesser, the Greater prevails. In each confrontation, Jesus was victorious. We conquer by His power which He has authorized us to use.

AUTHORITY OVER DEATH
Christ was falsely accused and wrongly tried. They mocked, scourged, tortured, and crucified Him. The soldiers would have chosen to make His grave with the wicked who were crucified with

Him. Instead, He was "with the rich in His death," so that Isaiah 53:9 could be fulfilled—for Joseph, a rich counselor, begged for His body to be buried in his own new tomb.

THE WONDER OF IT ALL

There were a number of miracles associated with His resurrection:

1. The wonder of the stone.

The stone was secured with Pilate's seal and Roman soldiers were on guard to watch over it, yet, according to Luke 24:2, the stone was rolled away from the sepulcher. It was not moved for Jesus to exit, but for the witnesses to see He had risen.

2. The wonder of the grave.

Luke 24:3 says they entered into the tomb and did not find the body of Jesus. He had been buried there, yet the tomb was now empty. The linen which had wrapped Him was lying in the same place and in the form as when the body was present, however, He was gone. The position of the clothes was clear evidence that no one had stolen the body. He was freed from a grave which was intended to confine Him and, in so doing, He freed us. The grave did not *contain* Him, but actually *glorified* Him.

3. The wonder of a vision.

Luke 24:4 records that two men stood by in shining garments. In following Jesus into the tomb, they were privileged to see the Glorified One. Every place Jesus had been was never again the same—even a dark and lonesome tomb.

4. The wonder of a message.

The angels asked Mary and Mary Magdalene why they were seeking the living among the dead. They informed the two women that Jesus was not there, He had risen. The angels also reminded them how Jesus had said, "The Son of Man must be delivered into the hands of sinful men, and be crucified, and the third day rise again." The message was, Jesus had been resurrected.

5. The wonder of disbelief.

The women left the tomb and told the apostles Jesus had risen. (Luke 24:10-11) This is a wonder in the sense it was astonishing that the apostles disbelieved. They certainly learned a lesson which launched them into greater faith and commitment.

6. The wonder of a conversation.

As two disciples on the Emmaus road communed together and reasoned concerning all that had happened, Jesus drew near and journeyed on with them (Luke 24:13). They did not know it was Jesus, so they began to tell Him about Himself! Jesus questioned whether Christ should have suffered these things and enter into glory. He spoke of Moses, the prophets, and the scriptures concerning Himself. He stayed and ate with them, and their eyes were opened. Their hearts "burned within them" as Jesus conversed.

7. The wonder of a Stranger.

They asked this Man, "Art thou only a stranger in Jerusalem?" (Luke 24:18). What words these were to be spoken to Jesus, the One who had been wounded and crucified for them. The One they thought was simply a stranger, was Jesus Himself.

THE MASTER CONQUEROR PROVIDED FOR US

One of the most powerful statements in the New Testament was written by the apostle Paul: *"I am crucified with Christ: nevertheless I live; yet not I, but Christ liveth in me: and the life which I now live in the flesh I live by the faith of the Son of God, who loved me, and gave himself for me"* (Galatians 2:20).

We live for God by being crucified with Christ. When a person believes Jesus died for him, that Jesus bore their sin, God takes the individual's faith and considers him as having died with Christ—identifying with the Lord in death. He looks at that person's faith as though he has already been punished for sin in the death of Christ.

From that moment on, we can live for God by allowing Christ to live His life through our bodies. We are to be so submitted to Christ as though He is walking upon the earth in *us*. This is significant:

- It means we will live as Christ lived.
- It means we will operate with the power He operated with.
- It means we will deal with demonic forces as He did.
- It means we will conquer as He did.
- It means we will succeed as He did.
- It means we can do all things through Christ.

THE RIGHT MINDSET

Conquerors are victors because they operate with the proper mindset. No one fails until failure takes place within them—and we must believe we are never defeated unless we defeat ourselves.

If you think you are beaten, you are. If you feel it is too hard, it is. If you think you'll lose, you will. You must be sure of yourself before you can ever achieve success. Remember, the successful person is not always the stronger, faster, more intelligent one, but ultimately they are those who think they can win.

Unhealthy Mindsets

Most people never experience a "conquering" lifestyle because they are operating in the wrong frame of mind. Let's examine some of these unhealthy mindsets:

1. A carnal mind.

"Because the carnal mind is enmity against God: it is not subject to the law of God, neither indeed can be" (Romans 8:7). This is a mindset which follows human nature—an earthly mind that is hostile and hateful toward the ways of God.

2. A blinded mind.

"In whom the god of this world hath blinded the minds of them which believe not, lest the light of the glorious gospel of Christ, who

is the image of God should shine unto them" (2 Corinthians 4:4). This is the thinking of those who are blind to the ways of God. The gospel is hidden from them and they operate in disbelief. Some believers wrongly allow themselves to be blinded to certain biblical truths.

3. A vain mind.
"This I say therefore, and testify in the Lord, that ye henceforth walk not as other Gentiles walk, in the vanity of their mind" (Ephisians 4:17) This is a mind which is occupied with things that pass quickly into and out of existence. It is the thought process of those who are caught up with the earthly existence, and whose understanding has been darkened.

4. A reprobate mind.
"And even as they did not like to retain God in their knowledge, God gave them over to a reprobate mind, to do those things which are not convenient" (Romans 1:28). (1 Peter 2:9). We are referring to a mind void of proper judgment-making ability and without principles. It is a mind worthless or rejected.

5. A defiled mind.
"Unto the pure all things are pure: but unto them that are defiled and unbelieving is nothing pure; but even their mind and conscience is defiled" (Titus 1:15). This is a contaminated mind that suffers from sin and pollution.

6. A doubtful mind.
"And seek not ye what ye shall eat, or what ye shall drink, neither be ye of a doubtful mind" (Luke.12:29). This is a mindset which lacks definite conviction. It fluctuates with anxiety and wars against our faith.

All of these mental attitudes work against us as we strive to achieve the fulfillment of our visions and dreams. Therefore, it is important not to allow ourselves to develop and operate with any of them. They do not promote our spiritual growth and development.

Healthy mindsets.

Thankfully, scripture points us to a better way of thinking. Here are a few of the healthy mindsets encouraged in scripture:

1. A renewed mind.

"And be not conformed to this world: but be ye transformed by the renewing of your mind, that ye may prove what is that good, and acceptable, and perfect will of God" (Romans 12:2). This is a spiritually renovated mind that comes as a result of our newly created spirit man. It removes conformity to this world and produces transformation to God's Kingdom.

2. A sound mind.

"For God hath not given us the spirit of fear; but of power, and of love, and of a sound mind" (2 Timothy 1:7). We are talking about a disciplined mind that produces self-control.

3. A lowly mind.

"Let nothing be done through strife and vainglory; but in lowliness of mind let each esteem other better than themselves" (Philippians 2:3). Here is a mindset that produces humility before God and others.

4. A ready mind.

"Feed the flock of God which is among you, taking the oversight thereof, not by constraint, but willingly; not for filthy lucre, but of a ready mind" (1 Peter 5:2). This mindset makes us immediately available to God.

THE MIND OF TRIUMPH

There are certain traits which dominate the thoughts of those who triumph in the face of adversity. The Lord has positioned us to achieve these attributes—which lead to continual victory. Here are six specific qualities which can be ours:

49

1. A delivered mind.

Our thoughts must be set free from the power and bondage of sin. The delivered mind is one which is removed from the enemy and given to the Lord's possession. It is lifted from the sinful position and placed in one of righteousness—no longer under the control of the flesh. Now it is guided by the Holy Spirit. We cannot conquer if we are already conquered, and a mind that is not *delivered* from worldliness cannot *overcome* worldliness.

2. A dedicated mind.

This is a mind set apart to God for specific Kingdom purposes. It is committed to the goals established by the Lord, delivered from sin's bondage and dedicated to the fulfillment of God's will. It is devoted to the worship of the Lord in word and deed. A mind dedicated to the Lord will produce actions which promote conquering.

3. A disciplined mind.

Our thoughts must be corrected, trained, and molded to be obedient. It's been said no evil propensity of the human heart is so powerful that it may not be subdued by discipline. The subjection of the mind is the process of bringing it under control—and maximized discipline comes by the power of the Holy Spirit.

4. A properly "dieted" mind.

A natural diet is the food and drink we consume to feed and maintain the vital functions of our bodies. Our minds must also have proper nourishment. The mental intake determines the state or condition of our thinking. This is why we must have a steady diet of the Word of God, godly meditation, clean conversation, good reading material, and music that promotes godly desire.

5. A developing mind.

The potential of the human brain is more than we will ever know. So we must constantly keep it open for learning and instruction—to develop its possibilities. A non-developing mind remains stationary like a parked automobile. In this state it does not accept data and is destined for defeat. On the other hand, the mind directed by God produces activities planned by Him.

6. A durable mind.

We need a mind which enables us to withstand hardship and suffering and is not easily discouraged—one that can take major blows and still continue. As Paul writes, *"For I am persuaded, that neither death, nor life, nor angels, nor principalities, nor powers, nor things present, nor things to come, nor height, nor depth, nor any other creature, shall be able to separate us from the love of God, which is in Christ Jesus our Lord"* (Romans 8:38).

THE POWER OF A WINNING ATTITUDE

What is your mental position toward succeeding and achieving? Do you maintain the necessary frame of mind to win?

It is easier to keep a winning attitude when we realize how blessed we already are. No matter what our state or condition, it could always be worse. The understanding of how favored we are allows us to resist discontentment, and complaining—and is a source of encouragement during hard times.

When we focus on God's love, it motivates us to work in His Kingdom and keeps our hope alive. Through it we have a manifestation of the work of the Lord in our lives which promotes our praise and worship.

We must also stop looking at what we *don't* have. The continual viewing of our lack encourages a negative attitude. It ignites discontentment, loss of focus and can cause depression, self-pity, and damaged confidence. It causes some to doubt the success of their future. Each test we pass helps prepare us for the removal of some of the lack in our lives. This is why we must concentrate on the good which currently exists in our lives; it will sustain us until better days arrive.

You may not live in a palace, but there is a place to stay. No companion, but friends. Not much money, but your needs are met.

51

Refuse to be Defeated

We must also remember that the loss of a battle is not the loss of the war. There will be times when we will experience hardship, even failure. Setbacks do not mean we are failures in life. Paul was beaten, stoned, imprisoned and persecuted, yet still declared that, as believers, we are more than conquerors. He realized his sufferings and reversals did not mean he was a loser. Even in the dark days of persecution, he was not defeated, saying, "I can do all things through Christ..."

Do all you can to launch forward—preparing yourself for victory in each situation. Regulate your thinking to be victorious and *purpose* to win. You can overcome obstacles through wisdom, prayer and fasting. Stand firm on God's Word and refuse to be defeated.

Are You Ready for the Challenge?

As Kingdom conquerors we do not think about why we *cannot,* but how we *can!* We must not complain because things are a little more difficult than we would like. Instead, we understand the best in us is developed by the resistance we encounter. It is clear we must accept the challenges of changing times and conditions if we are to fulfill our God-given purposes.

Too many are seeking ways to avoid challenges. It has been said the world can be divided into three classes: the few who *make* things happen, the many who *watch* things happen, and the overwhelming majority who have no notion of what happens! We determine the category we will be in by the way we conduct our lives.

Throughout scripture we find amazing examples of God's people facing the mountains that were set before them.

- Moses met the challenge of Pharoah's resistance to releasing the Israelites.
- Joshua met the challenge of leading Israel into Canaan and in the overthrow of Jericho.
- Deborah and Barak met the challenge of King Jabin and the captain of his host, Sisera.
- Samson met the ultimate challenge of the Philistines.

- Daniel met the challenge of the lions den.
- Jehoshaphat met the challenge of Moab and Ammon.
- Gideon met the challenge of the Midianites.
- Elijah met the challenge of the false prophets.

From these challenges and more, we can learn some valuable truths:

1. They are to build us up, not to tear us down.

We must find a way to handle obstacles in a manner which will promote rather than demote us. When they arise, we must purpose to turn them into launching pads. We must *meet* them and *beat* them, and make them stepping stones to better things. They are for our benefit.

2. They provide valuable experience.

The lessons of today's challenges will enable us to win tomorrow's victories. Our experiences teach us what, when, where, and *how* to do. By them we discover healthier ways to conduct our lives through the increase of the wisdom and knowledge gained.

In acquiring experience, we should focus not only upon what happens to us, but also on what we do with the knowledge of what has taken place. It is important to analyze what we go through and benefit from these findings. If I made a bad decision, I want to know the details so I will not repeat the same mistake again. Also if I made a good decision, I want to discover the facts so I can make wiser choices.

3. They manifest our strengths and weaknesses.

There are times when we either overestimate or underestimate our abilities. It is important for us to know the reality of who we are as well as the extent of our abilities. The knowledge of our strengths and weaknesses enables us to act wisely when we are challenged. Such data keeps us from falling into unnecessary traps. It helps us to discover the areas of our lives which need to be strengthened or improved.

53

4. They build our faith.
It is through our walk with the Lord we come to know and trust Him. The more we learn, the greater our faith and confidence in Him. It is necessary to fully believe we can depend on the Lord. Challenges test our faith—and strengthen our belief.

5. They enable us to build quality character.
As we learn from our encounters and apply them, our character will be improved. This is a foundation which will support the towering structure of our lives. Simply stated, character can be defined as the traits that make up and distinguish an individual. It exerts power over external circumstances, bending them in the right direction. It defies hardship, opposition, situations, circumstances and all types of challenges to produce a quality result.

DAVID WASN'T INTIMIDATED
In a time of confrontation, Israel was being threatened by one of its arch foes, the Philistines (1 Samuel 17). The enemies' camp was situated on the southern slopes of the valley of Elah and the Israelites were encamped three miles east.

Israel was being intimidated by the giant, Goliath. He called for Saul and the Israelites to choose a man to come out against him, one on one.

Among ancient Greeks, matters of war were sometimes settled by representative battles. The champion from each side would fight to settle the dispute. In this case, the Israelites were reluctant to go out against this man who was unequaled in height, standing nine feet or more tall. The magnificence of his brass helmet, armor and weapons made him appear to be invincible. They were fearful.

What situation currently has you quaking and intimidated? Perhaps it is a painful memory of abuse that will not go away. Maybe it is the consistent reminder of failed relationships. It could be the devastating death of a close relative or friend. Some of you may be suffering from a terminal illness, unexpected marital divorce, family rejection, the loss of a home by foreclosure, heavy financial debt, or the failure of a business.

FIGHTING FOR A CAUSE

We must seek to handle our situations as David handled his. When the men of Israel saw Goliath, they fled from him and were extremely afraid. However, it is not the intention of the Lord for us to run from our problems—because He is always with us.

Challenges are to be faced with the right mindset. David's older brothers, Eliab, Abinadab, and Shammah had gone to battle and David's father sent him to take some food to them on the field of war. Just as the Israelites were preparing to fight, he came to the trench and greeted his brothers As he talked to them, Goliath once again came out to taunt them as he had done for forty days.

As the men of Israel fled from him in fear, David asked what reward would be offered to the man who killed Goliath. They told him the king would bestow on that person great riches and would give the hand of his daughter.

David's brother, Eliab, heard his discussion with the men and became angry with him, asking, "Why did you come down here, and with whom did you leave the sheep?" He told David that he knew his pride and haughtiness of heart, and accused him of simply coming down to watch the battle. David responded, "Is there not a cause?"

You see, David was not really interested in the situation to receive the reward the king was offering. His purpose extended beyond Saul, and all the benefits—even beyond all of the men of Israel. David's cause was the *Lord's* cause!

A DIVINE PURPOSE

As we strive to conquer in our personal lives, we must view our efforts as seeking for the Lord's desires and purposes.

Jesus came to seek and to save those who are lost, to destroy the works of the devil, to preach, heal, and to liberate. Today, we are His people and He uses us to achieve His cause.

The activities of our lives are related to His divine purpose. This means enemy challenges are not only aimed toward us, but also the Lord.

David knew that when the Philistines came against Israel, they were coming against the Lord, because the Israelites were God's people. He was concerned over what the Lord desired, not his own interests.

Challenges are to be faced with faith. When the men heard how boldly David spoke for the Lord's cause, they told Saul, and he called for David. He informed Saul that no man's heart should fail, because he would go and confront the giant.

Saul told David he was not able to fight Goliath because he was still young—and the giant was a man of war from his youth. However, the Lord will use anyone He chooses, and the odds or enemy advantages do not matter.

David explained to Saul how he had defeated a lion and a bear when they came against the sheep of his flock. He told the king that Goliath would be as the lion or bear, because he had defied the armies of the living God. David said as the Lord had delivered him from those dangerous animals, He would surely deliver him out of the hand of Goliath.

THE BATTLE IS THE LORD'S

David's statement reflected his faith and he could see victory before the fight ever began because his belief removed any doubt concerning Goliath's defeat. Even the fear of death was gone.

Saul gave David his armor and placed a helmet of brass upon his head. But David refused to use the armor because he had never done so before. When we are challenged, we must use proven approaches to victory such as prayer, fasting, the exercise of faith, and the use of our God-given gifts, skills, and abilities. Adversity must be faced with boldness.

David took the staff in his hand and chose five smooth stones out of the brook, and put them in his shepherd's bag. He had learned to use his sling while tending his father's sheep and was not afraid. Those who defy the living God are not to be feared by those who trust Him. They are as windbags who cannot stand before the Almighty, a consuming fire.

When Goliath came out and saw little David for the first time, he laughed and regarded him as insignificant. David was young, reddish, and looked nothing like a warrior. The giant told David to approach him and he would give his flesh to the fowls of the air and beasts of the field. David responded, *"You come with a sword, spear, and a shield, but I come in the name of the Lord of hosts, the God of the armies of Israel you have defied. This day the Lord will deliver you into my hands. I will smite you and take your head off, and give the carcases of the Philistines to the fowls of the air and wild beasts that all may know there is a God in Israel. All here will know that God saveth, but not with the sword and spear. The battle is the Lord's and he will give you into our hands"* (1 Samuel 17:45-47).

Kingdom conquerors are fearless and their words reflect their confidence. David took off and ran toward Goliath and the Philistine army. He moved forward with invisible armor because he went in the name of the Lord—encased in a tower of strength. The only weapons he carried were a sling of faith and a stone of truth.

David released the stone from his sling and it hit and sunk into the forehead of Goliath who fell upon the earth, face down. David walked over, stood upon Goliath, withdrew the giant's sword and cut off his head. The Philistines fled, and Israel pursued them. Young David faced the challenge and was victorious.

BROKEN VESSELS

To conquer we must be broken and flexible in the hands of God. Resistance within us must disappear so we can carry out His directives. Those who become mighty in the Lord are those who can be molded by Him. We see this brokenness in David—and it allowed the Lord to take him to higher levels.

Remember:

- It was from a broken rock that water came in the wilderness for Israel.
- It is broken ground which opens its bosom for the reception of the seed that will bring forth fruit.
- It is broken clouds which discharge showers.
- It was from the broken alabaster box the penitent woman anointed Jesus' feet.

- It is Christ's broken body which furnished the blood that cleanses the soul.
- It is the broken veil that opens into the Holy of Holies.
- It is the broken grave that announces the reality of the resurrection.

When our resistance to the commands of the Lord are removed, He can then bless us as He desires. We must be broken because portions of our being resist releasing earthly activities and we must lose our desire for the things of the world.

KINGDOM CONQUERORS PERSEVERE
Despite opposition, we must learn to press forward with determination.

Our perseverance reflects a deepened love for God.
There are many Christians who claim they love the Lord, and perhaps they do, but they are hesitant to endure for Him. However, those who have walked with Him and developed a deepened love will press on.

It's been said, "Those who truly love are but one step from heaven. Our love for God is stronger than the things that come against us." We do not love the Lord so we can *get* from Him, we love Him and desire to *give* to Him.

We worship the Lord so much that we live for Him, labor for Him, give our tithes and offerings to Him, and value Him more than anyone or anything else. Our deep adoration for the Lord produces unwavering faith, entire submission, graceful humility, patient suffering, active serving and steadfast loyalty.

Our perseverance reflects a decided mind.
We are free from doubt or hesitation and push on because we have a "made up" mind. Since we are with Christ, there is no doubt we are where we want to be—and will never leave. Our minds are immovable because we have knowledge of the Lord, with experience that has increased our desire to abide and rest in Him. Regardless of

what is swirling around us, we stand strong because we have decided to follow Him.

Our perseverance reflects our desire to defeat the enemy. Scripture tells us we are to resist our adversary the devil (1 Peter 5:10). This is necessary because a major goal of the enemy is to hinder and stop the work of believers. It takes much perseverance to defeat his tricks, schemes, devices, traps and temptations. The devil must be defeated because he comes only to steal, kill, and destroy. So we are to rebuke and defy him every step of our earthly journey.

Our perseverance reflects our determination to achieve. It is the desire of the Lord that we triumph in all areas of our lives. This is why we must "keep on keeping on."

- Jacob wrestled the Lord and was determined to get his blessing.
- Joshua was determined and Jericho was defeated.
- Samson was determined and defeated the Philistines.
- David was determined and defeated Goliath.
- Jehoshaphat and Judah were determined and defeated the Ammonites.
- Nehemiah was determined and the Jerusalem wall was completed.

A VESSEL NAMED PAUL

The apostle Paul's life manifests a process that produces Kingdom conquerors. He progressed from a persecutor of Christians to a defender of the faith. His steps to achievement are much like the ones we must take today.

Initially, Paul was an unclean vessel. He lashed out threatenings and slaughter against God's people. Like us, he was born in sin and shaped in iniquity. Though we were predestined to do God's work, we were born in sin. Paul was a blasphemer and a persecutor of God's people early on, but the Father's

59

mark was upon him.

I often reflect on my life before I came to Christ because it causes me to more clearly realize that His hand was on my life. We are moving to our predestined places in Christ and nothing can stop us. That is why mothers could not abort us, ghetto drive-bys could not kill us, and drugs and alcohol could not destroy us before Christ. We were unclean, but He protected and preserved us. As defiled vessels, we were liars, cheats, adulterers, fornicators, rejecters of the truth, lawbreakers, and some were good people, but without Christ.

Paul became an empty vessel.

When the Lord confronted him on the road to Damascus, Paul questioned Him, asking, "Lord what wilt thou have me to do?" He abandoned his former life. When he was emptied, he forsook his own plans and purposes.

As Kingdom conquerors, we must empty ourselves and give all to God. The Lord turned Paul upside down and emptied him of his sin. We must be progressively freed of the ungodliness or worldliness within us.

Paul was a chosen vessel.

The Lord instructed Ananias to go to the street called Straight to pray for Paul so he could receive his sight. He told Ananias, Paul was a chosen vessel unto Him. Paul was selected before the foundation of the world, but now he was about to be further prepared for his earthly assignment. We have also been chosen by the Lord to fulfill our Kingdom role, and to conquer.

Paul became a filled vessel.

When Ananias laid his hands upon Paul, he was filled with the Holy Spirit (Acts 9:17). It is the power of the Spirit which allows us to conquer. He provides the anointing for our assigned Kingdom functions, leads and guides us in our predestined path, makes intercession and enables us to experience genuine, sincere prayer. There was much in Paul's future that would require him to be a conqueror. To do so, he had to be Spirit filled and empowered.

Paul became a separated vessel.

As the believers ministered to the Lord in Acts 13, the Holy Spirit instructed those present to separate Barnabus and Paul for the work they were called to do. Paul began the book of Romans by saying, *"Paul, a servant of Jesus Christ, called to be an apostle, separated unto the gospel of God."* Full use by the Lord requires that we remove ourselves from the world system so He can separate us unto the work He has called us to. It is the separated life that promotes spiritual growth for greater use by the Lord.

Paul was a suffering vessel.

He conquered because he learned to endure persecution. In 2 Corinthians 11:23-27, Paul catalogued his sufferings as perils of waters, robbers, his countrymen, the city, the wilderness and false brethren. He said he was troubled on every side, but not distressed or upset. He was perplexed, yet not in despair. He was persecuted, but not forsaken, cast down, yet not destroyed. It is encouraging to know that if we successfully endure our suffering, we will experience the fulfillment of our dreams and visions.

Paul was a praying vessel.

His communion with the Lord was constant, consistent, and continual. He conquered because he prayed. The scriptures reveal Paul's commitment to prayer (1 Thessalonians 5:17; Romans 1:9; 1 Corinthians 1:4). We win because we have learned how prevailing prayer brings perpetual power. It is the intimacy with the Lord which is necessary to meet, beat, and conquer all that oppose us.

Paul was an honored vessel.

He was honored by being used of God to open the eyes of many, and turn them from darkness to light, from the power of Satan unto God. He penned fourteen books of the New Testament.

Paul became a finished vessel.

We cannot complete our course in a manner that pleases the Lord if we do not become conquerors. In 2 Timothy 4:6-7, Paul writes:

"For I am now ready to be offered, and the time of my departure is at hand. I have fought a good fight, I have finished my course, I have kept the faith." In the completion of his work, he had walked the earthly portion of his path, and finished his earthly assignment. He had conquered.

We must never forget that divine destiny is attached to our lives. The Lord has placed in us all we need to both fulfill His desires and to make a dynamic difference in this world.

With God's help, you can do it!

CHAPTER 3

DOWN, BUT
NOT DEFEATED

*And Jacob dwelt in the land wherein his father
was a stranger, in the land of Canaan. These are the generations
of Jacob. Joseph being seventeen years old,
Was feeding the flock with his brethren; and the lad was
with the sons of Bilhah, And with the sons of Zilpah, his father's
wives: and Joseph brought unto his father their
evil report. Now Israel loved Joseph more than all his children,
because he was the son of his old age:
and he made him a coat of many colours.*
– GENESIS 37:1-3

*And it came to pass, when Joseph was come
unto his brethren, that they striped Joseph out of his
coat, his coat of many colours that was on him. And
they took him, and cast him into a pit: and the
pit was empty, there was no water in it.*
– GENESIS 37:23-24

However you define success—wealth, fame or the favorable
outcome of an undertaking—most people fall short.

While the focus of this book is on achievement, I firmly believe
that spiritual success, when accomplished God's way, will promote
winning in other areas of life. Why? Because biblical principles are
universal.

Even though some believers are uncomfortable with the topic, I feel it is important to discuss subjects such as success and prosperity. There are those who feel a life of abundance is not for the Christian—that our earthly walk should be one of continual struggle with minimal rewards. Even more, they measure spiritual strength by their ability to endure and survive their problems.

TRUE SUCCESS

After years of observation, I've come to the conclusion that many struggle because they simply choose to. I also believe the Lord has provided a plan for us which will bring total prosperity—one that gives the highest priority to the spiritual, but does not reject health, family, career, and economic favor, as well as prosperity in other areas of life.

Some say success is relative, that one cannot measure the achievement of an individual by comparing their status to others—that the true measure of success is realized when we see where the person was and where they are now.

It's true we all have various levels of gifts and talents, and individuals with greater ability will accomplish more. Others who achieve less can, in actuality, be more successful than those who accomplish more, because in the process of achieving they used their abilities to a greater extent.

This being the case, true achievement is measured by gauging the scope to which we utilize what God has given us, not by comparing ourselves with others. Many have finances because of inheritance, yet it doesn't mean they are successful. If they fail to manage their money wisely, they could end up broke!

Some who read these words are in the midst of turmoil. Perhaps it is a troubling time and you cannot see any breakthroughs leading to a time of triumph. My friend, you may feel down and defeated, yet in reality you are not. The Lord has sent me to tell you there is a way out of your current dilemma.

Your Heavenly Father wants you to succeed, but it starts with the basics. In fact, you must travel the path of toil and labor.

Unfortunately, a large number of believers come to Christ looking for pie in the sky and an instant outpouring of blessings upon their lives. It simply does not work this way. Success comes lesson after lesson from the teacher, blow after blow of the laborer, crop after crop of the farmer, picture after picture of the painter, rehearsal after rehearsal and practice after practice for the musician, and step after step for the dancer.

WHY WE FAIL

We will not reach the high levels and accomplish what we desire without putting in preparation time. Triumph is not guaranteed by doing only what is necessary, but by doing *more* than is required. It comes to people who do not mind long hours and are willing to put in the time to accomplish and achieve what they are striving for. It's been said, "The only time success comes before work is in the dictionary!"

Author Napoleon Hill analyzed several thousand people and said ninety-eight percent of them were considered failures. So he conducted another study to learn *why* those persons failed. He discovered their lack of success was due to the fact they had one or more of the following conditions prevailing in their lives:

1. An unfavorable hereditary background.
2. A lack of a well-defined purpose.
3. Insufficient education.
4. A lack of self-discipline.
5. Ill health.
6. Unfavorable environmental influences.
7. A lack of persistence.
8. A negative personality.
9. A lack of control of sexual urges.
10. Uncontrolled desire for receiving something for nothing.
11. Poor decision making.
12. Overcome by one of the six basic human fears:
    Fear of criticism.

Fear of sickness.
Fear of a loss of love.
Fear of old age.
Fear of poverty.
Fear of death.
13. Wrong mate selection for marriage.
14. Overly cautious.
15. Wrong choice of business associates.
16. Superstition and prejudice.
17. A lack of concentration.
18. Wrong selection of vocation.
19. Inability to cooperate and work with others.
20. Possession of power that was not personally achieved.
21. Intentional dishonesty.
22. Egotism and vanity.
23. Guessing instead of thinking.
24. A lack of capital.

I am asking you to take a realistic assessment of where you are during this particular time in your life. Then ask yourself, "Why am I here?"

In practically every case, our present situation is the result of the actions we have taken. In other words, if you are not successful today, it is because of the things you have done in your yesterdays.

The responsibility for our current status essentially rests with each of us—even though it is often convenient to blame other factors.

Here's the next reality. If we continue to do what we have always done, we will remain where we are.

STEPS TO ACHIEVEMENT

How do we get back on track?

First: It is important that where we are truly reflects the ability the Almighty has given us.

We must know our purpose and be sure we are using our

God-given talents to fulfill the dream.

Second: We must know why we are at our current place in life.

We must do more than simply complain, "I am not where I want to be." Again, ask, "Why?" This knowledge is invaluable so we can intelligently make the needed changes, adopting new ways of doing things which will bring the desired results.

What a waste to simply repeat the same mistakes or bad patterns of behavior. For example, if mortgage money is used for something other than the mortgage, the banker will threaten to, and eventually take your house. We must learn from experience and correct our behavior.

Third: We must know where we are going.

We cannot afford to drift through life aimlessly. As believers, the knowledge of our purpose in God's plan sets a course for us. Then, when we know where we are going, we can properly prepare for the journey. This also enables us to better understand some of the current tests we are going through and view them as preparation ordained by God.

Knowing our purpose allows us to properly set related goals that will aid us in gauging our progress. Each of us should set objectives for where we are going, spiritually and naturally. We must then use our God-given abilities to achieve those goals.

Fourth: We must discover what it will take to get there.

If we know where we are and where we are headed, we can determine a route to get there.

As believers in Christ, success is ours. It is okay to pursue higher education, own your own business and seek to move up the corporate ladder. If we place God first, He is going to open doors and prosper us. Our employers do not control our destinies. They only have the power over us that God allows them to have and, at the appointed time He will promote us.

It is perfectly permissible for a believer to achieve both spiritual and financial stability—including investing in the stock market and mutual funds. Why would God have Jesus endure all He went through and then not want the best possible life for His people? The Bible says, *"Beloved, I wish above all things that thou mayest prosper and be in health, even as thy soul prospereth"* (3 John 2).

TOTAL ABUNDANCE

If God brings prosperity to our souls, He will bring *total* prosperity to our lives. If we are faithful to the first, the second will follow. Instead of worrying over mundane matters, we should seek God and allow our souls to prosper. It will bring benefits to other areas of our walk.

Paul writes, *"Blessed be the God and Father of our Lord Jesus Christ, who hath blessed us with all spiritual blessings in heavenly places in Christ"* (Ephesians 1:3).

These spiritual blessings are of the Holy Spirit and are eternal, not temporal. They are greatly superior to earthly blessings and can only be found in Christ. Our identification with Him enables us to receive this outpouring of His favor. I am not saying every believer is going to be materially rich, rather they will experience total prosperity.

If our spiritual health pleases the Lord, we are spiritually successful already and, if we do things properly, we will achieve total abundance.

BLESSINGS FOR BELIEVERS

Paul reveals some vital truths concerning believers in Ephesians chapter one. Let's take a look at them.

1. The Lord has blessed us.
"Blessed be the God and Father of our Lord Jesus Christ, who hath blessed us with all spiritual blessings in heavenly places in Christ" (Ephesians 1:3).

2. The Lord has chosen us.
"According as he hath chosen us in him before the foundation of

the world, that we should be holy and without blame before him in love" (v.4).

Before the creation of the world, the Lord determined to have believers who would be in Him, holy, and without blame. He knows every human thoroughly and completely, but still He chose us. In God's divine process, He alone knows His total plan and every need He must fulfill in order for it to succeed—and every individual He will need to carry out His plan. We were chosen in Him before the foundation of the world and He placed within us all He would need to use at His appointed time.

At our birth, we simply stepped into our earthly existence to start developing as He predetermined. He did not just *happen* to choose us, but He did based upon His omniscience. The fact we are chosen means there is goodness in us to be developed. It tells us God's plan is favorable—and so will be our outcome. It lets us know we will prosper in our undertakings, and that we have potential not yet tapped into. When opposition rises against us, it will fall before us, because when we step out by faith, He will sustain us.

3. The Lord has predestined us.

"Having predestinated us unto the adoption of children by Jesus Christ to himself, according to the good pleasure of his will" (Ephesians 1:5).

The word predestination means "to destine"or appoint before, or to foreordain. It has been decided that we become children of God through adoption. We can overcome all that rises against us and all things work together for our good. We have the ability to stand in the liberty Christ has provided for us. Not only will we be successful in this life, but will spend eternity with Christ.

4. The Lord has accepted us.

"To the praise of the glory of his grace, wherein he hath made us accepted in the beloved" (Ephesians. 1:6). He has extended His grace toward us and we have become highly favored. The sacrifice of Christ positioned us to be accepted.

5. The Lord has redeemed us.

"In whom we have redemption through his blood, the forgiveness of sins, according to the riches of his grace" (v.7).

"Redemption" is a key word in the Bible. It conveys the concept of deliverance or setting a person free by paying a ransom. In our society people are sometimes kidnaped and money has to be paid to obtain their freedom. Man was held captive by Satan and sin, and was powerless to free himself, but God has redeemed man by the blood of Jesus Christ. When a person sincerely turns to the Lord, God purchases him right out of the marketplace of sin. Through Christ's blood sacrifice we have received forgiveness of iniquity according to the riches of God's grace.

6. The Lord has abounded to us in all wisdom.

"Wherein he hath abounded toward us in all wisdom and prudence" (v.8).

The word wisdom means seeing and knowing what to do—the proper use of knowledge. It grasps life's great truths and sees the answers to the problems and situations. "Prudence" denotes seeing how to use and "do" the truth, knowing the direction to take. He has given us an abundance of wisdom and its proper use will bring success.

7. The Lord has made known to us the mystery of His will.

"Having made known unto us the mystery of his will, according to his good pleasure which he hath purposed in himself" (v.1:9).

A mystery is a truth revealed by the Father which had never before been known. It is unlocked to man at God's appointed time and we are privileged with this divine revelation of truth.

8. The Lord has given us an inheritance.

"In whom we have obtained an inheritance, being predestinated according to the purpose of him who worketh all things after the counsel of his own will" (v.11).

We have been made the heritage of God and now belong to Him.

9. The Lord has sealed us with the Holy Spirit.

"In whom ye also trusted, after that ye heard the word of truth, the gospel of your salvation: in whom also, after that ye believed, ye were sealed with that Holy Spirit of promise, Which is the earnest of our inheritance until the redemption of the purchased possession, unto the praise of his glory" (vv.13-14).

The word *earnest* means "pledge, guarantee, or down payment." The Holy Spirit guarantees the assurance of the promises of the Father. We know we are God's by the Spirit who lives in us.

YOUR ASSIGNMENT

I am convinced the success and prosperity of believers is directly tied to the fulfillment of their God-given Kingdom assignments—and we have been equipped by the Lord to fulfill them.

When considering the value of life, how can any sane person allow it to pass without achievement? I am saddened to see so many individuals who seem to be going nowhere, drinking, drugging and partying their lives away. Others practically live on the street corners of American cities, unemployed, unconcerned and unfulfilled. Still others become wrapped in the scourge of homelessness, settling for much less than they are capable of producing.

It should be clear to every believer that we have been born and equipped before the foundation of the world to make a difference. The fulfillment of our assignments will produce a Kingdom enhancing impact which will not only benefit us but others as well.

- Noah was assigned the task of building the ark for use by the Lord in saving eight souls for the replenishing of the earth.
- Moses was called by the Lord to lead Israel out of Egyptian bondage, and to be one of God's greatest leaders.
- Joshua was assigned the task of succeeding Moses as the leader of Israel, and to lead them into Canaan.
- Joseph was given the assignment of sustaining God's people

71

during a major famine.
- David was assigned to be a king over Israel at a critical time in its history.
- Amos, Hosea, and Ezekiel were assigned to prophesy to Israel.
- Jonah and Nahum were assigned to prophesy to Nineveh.
- Daniel was assigned to prophesy to Babylon.
- Obadiah was assigned to prophesy to Edom.
- Joel, Isaiah, Micah, Jeremiah, Habakkuk, and others were assigned to prophesy to Judah.
- Apostle Peter was assigned to be a leader among the disciples and to preach the first message on the Day of Pentecost (Acts 2).
- Apostle Paul was called to evangelize the world and for extensive ministry to the Gentiles.

We have a calling—our vocation in the body of Christ. It is the area of ministry labor for which the Lord has equipped and sanctified us. To sanctify is also to make ready beforehand, so prior to the time we were born, the Lord prepared us for what He had called us to do. The question then arises, if we were prepared before we were born, why do we need to go through so much training to work in our calling? Why can't we simply step into our mission?

Well, God's preparation is His *equipping* of us with the necessary skills, gifts and abilities to effectively function in what He has planned. Joseph, as we will see, operated in his calling in a magnificent way. On the surface it may have appeared he was not capable of achieving to such a high degree of success, yet he was.

THE DREAMER!

Joseph was the eleventh of Jacob's twelve sons, and the firstborn son of Rachel. He was born in Padanaram when his father was ninety years old, and his father's favorite child because he was born of Rachel and the son of his old age. His father's favoritism was shown when he gave Joseph a coat of many colors, which probably was a token of rank indicating it was his father's intention to make him the head of the tribe. This gift caused much ill will between Joseph and his brothers.

Since Joseph was blessed to be a part of a wealthy family, some may wonder why I would use him as an example. But his story shows how far a person can fall—then rise again.

One day, Jacob sent Joseph to the field to see how his brother's were doing. When they saw him coming, they plotted to kill him, but Reuben suggested that they cast him into a pit—so he could return later and take Joseph back to their father. But by the time Reuben returned to the pit, his brothers had sold Joseph to the Ishmaelites for twenty pieces of silver. They, in turn, sold Joseph into slavery in Egypt. Now he was a homeless slave, separated from his family.

Joseph's handling of his situation reflected the quality of his character. He was resilient, with strength, and drive. He persevered and was determined to survive.

We cannot roll over in despair and allow every obstacle to stop us. Joseph could have said, "It's finished and I will never accomplish anything." But he chose to stay strong.

No More Excuses

I have seen people face life with a defeatist attitude, thinking they will never amount to much because their family was too far down the success ladder—too many school dropouts, failures, police records. Or it could be that no one ever encouraged or believed in them.

If I had used such excuses, I wouldn't be writing this book today. Remember, I came from a poor family and had a longstanding relationship with beans, fat back, powdered eggs and powdered milk. Even though I was raised in the projects, I never told myself I would stay there forever!

I remember the day my father told me he was sorry he did not have the finances to send me to college. He had spent all he could afford to put my older brother through university and I told him I understood completely. However, since I had personal goals, I would not allow a family situation to change by dream.

I cannot tell you how many paychecks left my hands for tuition and books, but I had a determined mind. I will never forget graduation day, and my father saying how proud he was of me.

When we walk with God, He will make provision. Instead of yielding to excuses, we must remember we are new creatures in Christ (2 Corinthians 5:17). We are fearfully and wonderfully made (Psalm 139:14). Our lives demonstrate His power (1 Corinthians 2:4). We can go boldly to the throne of grace when we need to (Hebrews 4:16).

THE BIRTH OF A VISION

Joseph had two dreams. In the first, he and his brothers were in the field binding sheaves—and his sheaf arose and stood upright. His brothers sheaves stood around his and bowed to his sheaf. You can imagine how his brothers hated him when they heard this, thinking he was superior.

In the second dream, the sun (his father), the moon (his mother), and eleven stars (his brothers) bowed down to him. When he shared this with Jacob and his brothers, his father rebuked him, yet observed and paid attention to what he said.

Joseph did not fully understand his dreams, but he knew they showed that somehow, somewhere, sometime his family would be under his authority. A vision was birthed in his life. It appeared that Joseph knew the dreams were from the Lord even though he did not relay it to his family with wisdom. We must be careful how and to whom we reveal our visions and dreams. Some will resent them. Others will be envious. Some will seek to hinder and discourage you. But there will be those who are glad and even help you to achieve your objectives.

Joseph believed in some unknown way the Lord was going to use him and provide all he needed in times of adversity.

It is important to seek God's vision for our lives. It will reveal where we are headed, what we will become and give us direction for the future. It also enables us to set goals and measure fulfillment. And during times of challenge, we can focus on our vision to motivate, drive and sustain us.

On our journey, we must never allow people or situations to become bigger than our dreams. If something is going wrong, seek God's help, apply the answer and move on.

We need to be so confident that we do not have to depend on outside reinforcement.

We cannot afford to allow the negative input of others to affect our thinking. Remember, not everyone will share the joy of our dream, but as long as we maintain our commitment, these things will not deter us.

THE TURNING OF THE TIDE

I stated earlier how Jacob sent Joseph out to check on his brothers and the flock. After a while he was successful in locating them, but that's when they conspired to kill him. His eldest brother, Reuben, told his brothers to shed no blood, but to simply cast Joseph into a pit. He planned to return, lift Joseph out and take him unharmed to his father. They stripped Joseph of his coat and cast him into that deep hole.

The brothers then killed a kid of a goat, dipped the coat in the fresh blood and brought it to their father, saying, "We found this and don't know if it is Joseph's."

Jacob immediately recognized the garment and concluded an evil beast had devoured his son. Jacob tore his clothes, put on sackcloth, and mourned for Joseph many days. All of his sons and daughters rose up to comfort him, but he refused to be consoled (Genesis 37:35). Jacob said he would go to his grave mourning the death of Joseph.

FACING "PIT" CONDITIONS

Joseph had been rejected by his brothers, had fallen from his position of wealth to one of poverty—cut off from family and friends. We also experience "pit" conditions, including the following:

1. *When we hit rock bottom.* Those times when it seems our lives have lost foundational support because so much has

gone wrong.

2. *When it appears everyone has forsaken us.* The moments we are facing extremely critical or life-threatening situations and no one is there to love or support us.

3. *When your spouse requests a divorce and walks out.* It is extremely painful to love someone deeply and have them walk out of the marriage unexpectedly.

4. *When there is an unexpected employment layoff.* These situations have caused some individuals to eventually lose their homes and other possessions.

5. *When a physician discovers you have a life-threatening condition.*

6. *When the infidelity of a spouse is discovered.*

7. *When a business fails and everything is lost.*

8. *When one becomes the victim of a crippling disease.*

9. *When a wife and newborn dies during delivery.*

10. *When a loved one becomes mentally unstable.*

These are only a few of the devastating situations which can cause us to reach a low valley in life. They may not seem as severe as Joseph's circumstances, but to those living through them, they are extremely challenging.

ADVANCING THROUGH ADVERSITY

Joseph knew how to face trials—which is reflected in the way he conducted himself during these dark days. The Bible does not indicate he fell apart and gave up. Instead, the sense of the scriptures is that he maintained his faith in the Lord and rested in the promises of God.

The people and events that work against us are the very things which strengthen us when we overcome them. With God's help, every believer must learn to deal with setbacks, disappointments, and failures; to face and handle what comes without allowing it to overwhelm or sink our faith. Also, we must not permit these forces to remove us from Kingdom activities and our praise and worship. It would be wonderful to go through life without struggle, but this desire is unrealistic.

As I often say, "The Lord *advances* us through adversity."

Joseph was a young man of good character. He loved the Lord and had been taught to revere and serve Him—and he also cherished and respected his family. As we will discuss later, many biblical scholars have portrayed him as a type of Christ: despised and rejected; a man of sorrow and acquainted with grief. Joseph was cast out by man, but was exalted by God to become a prince and savior. And it the midst of his adversity, Joseph maintained his integrity.

There is no indication in scripture Joseph turned away from the Lord or rejected Him. His hard times did not destroy him, rather they served to build his faith. His strength and excellence of character were manifested by the godly manner in which he faced and handled his many challenges.

Character is a key to victorious living—producing both quality work and a quality life:

- Through Noah's character the ark was built.
- Through Abraham's character a nation was formed.
- Through Joseph's character God's people were sustained through a famine.
- Through Moses' character the nation of Israel was brought out of Egypt.
- Through Joshua's character Israel was led into Canaan.
- Through Esther's character the nation of Israel was spared.
- Through David's character Israel was reunited.
- Through Peter's character the gospel was first taken to the Gentiles.
- Through Paul's character the gospel was continually preached to the Gentiles.

These individuals were used by the Lord because they possessed what was necessary for the performance of their assigned tasks:

- They loved the Lord and walked in His commandments.
- They were dedicated to the fulfillment of their purposes and callings.
- They labored diligently, and were constant and dependable.
- They placed the desire of the Almighty above their own personal wishes.
- They were anointed by the Lord and bold in the performance of their God-given tasks.
- They continued their engagement in the work of the Lord until He indicated their end had come.

We must be of exemplary character in the face of negative circumstances because they have a place in our growth and development.

A LEARNING EXPERIENCE

At the time we are immersed in problems, we can't understand why, yet there are benefits to "pit" situations:

1. They can bring divinely appointed isolation.

The quietness of our confinement provides the Lord with the opportunity to deal with us one-on-one. It is where God moved Joseph from fatherly favoritism and brotherly hatred to divine development. What may seem unfair can actually be the plan of God being carried out. The Lord sometimes allows us to encounter these conditions to position us for greater communion with Him.

2. They can teach us to lean upon the Lord for ourselves.

One of the most difficult things about pit situations is that they are often structured in a manner that others cannot assist us. This means we must learn to personally lean on God. Too often believers depend on their pastors, church leaders, and church members, but as they spiritually mature, there will come a time when they must learn to go to the Lord for themselves.

3. They manifest the true nature of our character.

Pit situations can be intense and emotionally draining. They are events which test us, and through them we can gain a true reflection of the type of person we really are. Sometimes they reveal things about us we are not aware of, mistakes we have made or changes we need to implement. Other times they show us how well we are doing.

4. They are obstacles that become stepping stones to our success.

We can be either stopped or hindered by pit situations, or we can turn them into stepping stones. They stand before us as obstacles to prevent us from advancing. If we allow them to block us, they will. But if we face them and learn from the experience, we can make the necessary adjustments and move forward.

5. They are under God's authority.

There are moments in God's orchestration of our lives He allows negative situations. On other occasions, we experience them because of our own doing. In either case, the Lord is always in control. This means we will not die in crisis. He will sustain us and use the lesson to further mold and shape us into His desired result.

ACTIONS TO TAKE

To rise from life's rough situations and develop quality spiritual character, we need a steady and consistent diet in the Word of God and the application of its principles.

The Word, if adhered to, will produce character of the highest caliber. After all, the Word *in* us will produce *from* us the life of Christ— which is our assurance of success and victory.

Joseph possessed the qualities we are discussing, and did not remain in his literal pit very long. I believe he was enlightened by his experience and this may have caused him to realize the extent of the hatred of his brothers toward him. Perhaps it allowed Joseph to understand how the talk concerning his dreams could have been dealt with differently—and that he did not handle his father's favoritism very well.

When we find ourselves in a similar situation, here are four things we can do:

First: We must master the opposition of the pit.

At times it appears the negatives of our lives have mastered us. The circumstances seems to dictate what we can or cannot do—and if we allow ourselves to be controlled by these events, our lives will become increasingly harder to bear.

Instead of giving up, we must, with God's help, maintain control and overcome. The actual mastering of a situation does not always entail leaving. We may not be able to alter what has taken place, but we can control it by changing the manner in which we view, deal with and allow it to affect us. In so doing, we don't let the event severely cripple us while we are waiting on the Lord to bring our deliverance.

Second: We must develop a "pit leaving" mentality.

The Lord did not save us to become confined to a pit. This means when problems surface they must not be allowed to imprison us. When we find ourselves trapped, we must possess a mentality which promotes our exit. Joseph could not move on with his life to perform and complete his assignment until he came out of the pit.

Our faith in the Lord assures us we will see the sun again. It causes us to visualize ourselves being delivered and gives us a new, positive vocabulary. We must constantly tell ourselves these problems will not always be part of our lives. If our trust and hope is in the Lord, He will honor His Word and come through for us.

Third: We must turn our pits into launching pads.

Discover, to the best of your ability, why the trouble exists. How did it come to pass? Why is God allowing this? What role is it playing in your development? Did you do something to cause the problem? What must you do to overcome? This is all a part of the process of mastering and leaving the pit and turning it into a launching pad.

Fourth: We must learn to sincerely worship the Lord.
Through all of our negative circumstances, we must continually worship the Lord. It reflects the nature of our spiritual walk and our love and faith in Him. Worship speaks of our assurance He will provide all we need to gain victory over the situation. Remember, He is still Lord, despite what is taking place.

In our worship we ascribe to God the glory due Him. Even when we are "down," we must celebrate the Lord, showing our appreciation for who He is and for all He has done.

AN EMOTIONAL ROLLER COASTER!

Joseph's brothers agreed to take him out of the pit, only to sell him to the Ishmaelite spice traders for twenty pieces of silver. This tells us even when we are languishing in a hole of despair, the Lord is making preparation for our exit—though we do not always know what lies ahead.

In Joseph's case, he left the prison of the pit only to enter the prison of slavery. What an emotional roller coaster!

To achieve success, we must understand we have been empowered by the Lord to overcome. *"But ye shall receive power after that the Holy Ghost is come upon you..."* (Acts 1:8). This is true even if we experience one devastating hit after another. *"...When the enemy shall come in like a flood, the spirit of the Lord shall lift up a standard against him"* (Isaiah 59:19).

We must continue even if we have a path of hurdles before us. *"Finally, my brethren, be strong in the Lord and in the power of his might"* (Ephesians 6:10).

If we can withstand the bombardment of attacks, we can receive a bounty of blessings. Each onslaught we overcome will strengthen our warfare base for the next volley. The attacks are proof of our strength because since God allows them, we can overcome.

Never forget Job, who suffered successive strikes from the enemy. He lost his servants, his flocks and his children, yet he still maintained his trust in the Lord. As Job responded, so must we.

A SEED OF POTENTIAL

We cannot afford to become preoccupied with circumstances because they are unpredictable. So instead of dwelling on occurrences which vary, we need to focus on the constancy of the Lord.

Joseph was sold to Potiphar, an officer of Pharaoh and captain of the guard. This man held an important position because he was in charge of protecting the life of Pharaoh.

The Bible tells us the Lord was with Joseph, and he prospered (Genesis 39:2). What a joy it is to have the Lord by our side through both our good and difficult times. Look at Joseph's story. He was a slave in a foreign land, separated from his family—isolated, neglected, rejected and forsaken. These circumstances are certainly not those which would promote success, yet the Lord had a plan for him.

God had planted a seed of potential in Joseph—a reservoir of future greatness.

Our potential is not determined by our history or background, but by the Lord. This being the case, our family lineage cannot erase or remove our hope. You see, it does not matter if our parents were Bonnie and Clyde, if our relatives were criminals or drug dealers, or if everyone around us operated in the realm of societal negativity, our potential remains what the Lord has placed inside each of us.

The realization of our possibilities lifts us up to God's preordained levels and promotes the expansion of His Kingdom. It increases our power over the enemy, reveals hidden strengths and makes us who God wants us to be.

"ACCORDING TO HIS PURPOSE"

Joseph's circumstances dictated failure, yet he flourished because he did not lose sight of the power of God—or the dream. He realized that situations can vary, but his faith was steadfast. This made it possible for him to stand strong in faith.

Potiphar saw that the Lord was with Joseph and made him overseer of his house. He put all that he had into Joseph's hand, and the Lord blessed Potiphar's house for Joseph's sake.

It is fascinating how the Lord continued to prepare Joseph in the midst of his undesirable environment. His appointment to leadership in Potiphar's house was God's way of preparing him for the fulfillment of his purpose. The Lord knew eventually Joseph would hold a prominent position in Egypt so He used this as a step in the process.

Some of our most trying times provide the greatest boost to our preparation. Joseph was facing hardship, but in the midst of it the Lord gave him a little relief. He not only resided in the comfort of Potiphar's home, he was named manager and had people under his authority.

Instead of being homeless, he had a roof over his head and clothes to wear. Technically, Joseph was a slave, but now he was a managing servant destined for bigger things.

If you have visions of what you desire to accomplish, do not allow your present condition to cause you to disqualify yourself. Your dream will be fulfilled because it is in God's plan. *"And we know that all things work together for good to them that love God, to them who are the called according to his purpose"* (Romans 8:28).

A DETERMINATION TO WORK

Joseph was not a lazy person. He rose to authority in Potiphar's house because he was a diligent worker and had the ability to perform the required tasks and to assume a high level of responsibility.

It's a law of nature that a certain quantity of work is necessary to produce a certain quantity of goods—of any kind whatever. If you want knowledge, you must labor for it; if you desire food, you must work for it; and if pleasure, you must toil for it. It only follows that if we want success, we must also work. As King Solomon observed, *"The hand of the diligent shall bear rule: but the slothful shall be under tribute"* (Proverbs 12:24).

Those who are determined and eager will rule. Those who are negligent in the performance of their duties, or not inclined to activity, shall be under domination, meaning they will be burdened in life.

"The soul of the sluggard desireth, and hath nothing: but the soul of the diligent shall be made fat" (Proverbs 13:4).

My parents taught me the importance of a good work ethic. During my childhood, they assigned certain chores to me and I was responsible for performing them properly and consistently. My father would always say, "If you are going to do a job, do it right. If not, don't do it at all."

My dad was quite a skilled and industrious person, and he achieved many things that would normally require a trained person. He learned:

- To be a barber and cut hair properly.
- To tailor clothes and made suits for us.
- To hang wallpaper and earned extra cash.
- Carpentry, plumbing, and electrical activities, and did these things well.
- To repair shoes and placed soles and heels on the shoes of family members.
- To be an excellent painter.
- To be a first-class gardener.

I was blessed to watch his activities and to be taught by him. In the process I developed a work ethic that has proven to be invaluable in all of my endeavors.

Success requires competence, consistency, dependability and a determination to work.

A MAN OF INTEGRITY

Joseph was promoted in Potiphar's house and undoubtedly was being well cared for. He was probably a well-dressed handsome young man who many of the women of the house found attractive. The Bible says *"...Joseph was a goodly person, and well favoured"* (Gensis 39:6).

Scripture records how Potiphar's wife cast her eyes upon Joseph as he went about his various duties. She was strongly attracted to him and allowed herself to lust after him. Then one day she approached Joseph and asked him to lay with her.

Joseph said to the woman, "How can I do this great wickedness, and sin against God?" (v.9).

He was a man of integrity and adhered to his spiritual code without compromise. Morally, he would not sleep with her and disrespect Potiphar. In spite of Joseph's response, she flirted and spoke to him daily in her vain attempts to entice him—yet he still refused.

The building of integrity is a process. Joseph did not draw from some ethical base which just happened to be within him at the moment. He became a person of integrity over a period of time as he committed himself to God and adhered to His word.

It is easy to succumb and follow our own desires, but living by moral principles requires we forego our feelings and obey God's laws and the proper codes of behavior. Romans 12:1 says we are to give ourselves as "living sacrifices" unto the Lord.

Our integrity is at the foundation of our spiritual walk. According to the Word, *"A just man walketh in his integrity: his children are blessed after him"* (Proverbs 20:7). We are also counseled, *"The integrity of the upright shall guide them: but the perverseness of transgressors shall destroy them"* (Proverbs 11:3).

Strict adherence to the Word assures us of His guidance and leads us in the paths of God's will. We must walk "unbending" in our integrity:

1. When wrongs are committed against us.
2. When dishonest acts bring career promotions.
3. When others receive positions we desire.
4. When others marry persons we desire.
5. When our names have been slandered.
6. When others fail to pay money owed to us.
7. When we have been caught in wrongdoing.
8. When we are severely criticized for things we have done.
9. When we arrive at points of desperation.
10. When we are offered a bribe to commit wrongdoings.

Joseph is a prime example of how to maintain our uprightness and integrity. He not only knew the statutes of the Lord, he walked in them. It was more important to please God than his carnal flesh.

A "WORST SITUATION" SCENARIO

Potiphar's wife persisted in her attempts to seduce Joseph. One day when none of the other men were in the house, she caught Joseph by his garment and again asked him to lay with her. He refused and fled, but as pulled away the garment was left in her hand..

Immediately, she called for some of the other servants and told them Joseph had forced his way into her bedroom to take advantage of her—and when she screamed, he fled. She even had the "evidence," the garment he left behind!

The conniving woman laid Joseph's garment beside her until Potiphar came home and once more she lied, giving the impression Joseph had attacked her. Potiphar became extremely angry and had the once-trusted Joseph put in the king's prison.

Falsely accused, his situation had deteriorated from better to worse and the conditions he now found himself in were deplorable. But he made the best of it.

Once he gathered his thoughts and pulled himself together, he remembered the dream and realized the favor of God was still upon him—and others must have recognized it too. It wasn't long before the warden of the prison was so impressed with Joseph that he made him keeper of the prisoners. Once again, the Lord was with him and he prospered.

Joseph did not wallow in self-pity, rather he was determined to do the best job possible in his new assignment.

When our lives take a downward spiral, we must continue our productive activities. This enables us to stay in touch with the value that lies within us. Too many times people count themselves out because something goes wrong in a particular area. Instead of giving up, we must learn to look at bad situations and discover ways to improve them.

We are sons and daughters of the King and although we are heavenly citizens living in an earthly abode, there will be negative encounters. But each time we face them we gain in strength and ability.

Joseph knew God had elevated his position in Potiphar's house, and believed He would help him again. I often wonder why so many believers are quick to forget the past assistance the Lord has provided. If He delivered us yesterday, He will do it again! We serve an immutable God who does not change. Joseph was content in a "worst situation" to rest in the will of God, and because he passed the test, he became the head of the prisoners.

THE BUTLER AND THE BAKER

The prison experience was teaching Joseph patience and endurance. He was learning to treat others properly, even during times of hardship and distress. Through all of this, the Lord still had a plan to cause Joseph to come to realize the gifts within him. This was manifested when, on a certain day, Pharaoh imprisoned his chief butler and baker. The butler was the one responsible for the king's vineyards and wines. He also served the king, and even tasted the wine, as cupbearer, to be sure it was not poisoned.

The baker's responsibility was the king's food. The reason for their imprisonment is not stated. Perhaps there was some infraction which caused them to be incarcerated pending investigation. Joseph, as head of the prisoners, was placed over these two men and cared for their needs. The Bible records they were all in prison for a season (Genesis 40:4).

God orchestrated the activities that placed Joseph over the butler and baker just as the Lord will bring people into our lives to carry out His plan for us. They can provide knowledge and guidance or use their influence to help us. Perhaps they will open doors to place us in the company of particular individuals.

Believers often do not see the hand of the Almighty operating in their circumstances because they are consumed with worry. We must never get so buried by our problems that we lose sight of the move of

God in our lives.

WHAT DOES THIS MEAN?

The Lord was about to act on Joseph's behalf and he was prepared. One night both the butler and the baker had a dream, and neither of them knew the interpretation. The chief butler saw a vine with three branches. It blossomed and clusters of grapes came forth. Pharaoh's cup was in the butler's hand and he pressed the grapes into Pharaoh's cup and gave it to him.

Since the age of 17, Joseph had been gifted in the interpretation of dreams and we are about to see how this ability played a vital role in his ultimate success.

Joseph told the butler what the dream meant—that in three days Pharaoh would restore him to his former position. He asked the butler to remember him and make mention of his name to Pharaoh, so he could be freed. This indicates the pressure was taking a toll on Joseph and he had a strong desire to be liberated.

The chief baker, in his dream, had three white baskets on his head. In the uppermost basket there were all types of "bakemeats" for Pharaoh and the birds ate them.

Joseph informed the baker that in three days Pharaoh would hang him and the birds would eat his flesh from his bones.

On the third day, the events occurred just as Joseph had predicted they would.

Our gifts and abilities are important and we must strive to know what they are. They will bless us in the things of Christ as well as in our natural careers. God places them in us so they can be used to fulfill His purpose for our lives, and for use as doors which lead to total prosperity. Primarily, however, they are designed for the expanding of God's Kingdom and to be a blessing to others.

THE SETBACK

On the third day Pharaoh restored the chief butler and hung the chief baker just as Joseph had interpreted the dreams. Remember,

Joseph had asked the chief butler to mention him to Pharaoh after he was freed, however, he failed to do so.

What a discouraging situation—to be ignored! It is difficult to see how the chief butler could have forgotten Joseph in view of the precision in his prediction of the butler's release. The miraculous nature of the word spoken by Joseph would cause most people to remember, but it obviously was not God's perfect time for Joseph's release.

From man's point of view, a delay lengthens the time it will take to rise to success. By our very nature, we want it "now." But from God's standpoint things are still on schedule. He knows more preparation is needed for the victory He is bringing.

When setbacks come, we must realize we are still operating on God's timetable.

Joseph handled his disappointment well and his passion for the Father caused him to endure all things. I like to think of our love for God as a gas mask in a gas-filled room, like an air tank in the depths of the ocean, like a water hose in a fire, like a glass of refreshing water in the middle of the desert, and like a protective cage in the middle of a pack of hungry, vicious wolves. In the words of the psalmist, *"...they shall prosper that love thee"* (Psalms 122:6).

During our earthly setbacks we must love the Lord even more.

PATIENCE AND PERSISTENCE

As a master of patience, Joseph had an innate ability to bear his pains and trials calmly and without complaint. After praying, we must endure our reversals with quiet expectation. Patience is the rope of faith to bring us back and it keeps us from acting prematurely or becoming disheartened with the Lord. It gets us through times of pain.

As Peter counsels, *"For this is thankworthy, if a man for conscience toward God endure grief, suffering wrongfully. For what glory is it, if, when ye be buffeted for your faults, ye shall take it patiently? But if, when ye do well, and suffer for it, ye take it patiently, this is acceptable with God"* (1 Peter 2:19-20).

Joseph's conduct was acceptable with the Lord because even

though he was wrongfully imprisoned, he demonstrated composure. Romans 12:12 says we are to be longsuffering in tribulation.

Patience cannot be snatched from its abstract setting, neither can it be given to us by others. It must be birthed inside of us through the seed of our desire and need. After birth, its ground must be fertilized to promote growth. The nutrients are prepared by a spiritual and natural agricultural specialist—the Lord Himself.

It is through testing that God prepares our soil so patience can grow. It makes us durable.

During hard times patience keeps us cheerful and in a positive state of mind. It helps us to stay spiritually grounded, fortified and focused on the Lord and enables us to continue our praise and worship. Our patience also allows us to possess what God has promised. The Word tells us, *"...be not slothful, but followers of them who through faith and patience inherit the promises"* (Hebrews 6:12).

Faith secures what we want. Hope causes us to expect it and patience keeps us in the walk with God until we receive it.

Joseph was persistent, staying on course despite all the interference he encountered. Persistence prevents quitting and builds a warrior-like spirit within us.

Joseph was also a master of perfection. I am using the term in the sense of maturity. He walked in a seasoned level of commitment, dedication, faith, patience, persistence, and passion. He had not achieved his full potential, yet he continued his advancement. Setbacks didn't deter him.

THE POWER OF A POSITIVE OUTLOOK

At times, happiness can seem to be as a fleeting jet, disappearing into the clouds.

The Lord desires that we live happily and successfully, but how do we handle all of the challenges?

When problems arise, some people act as if their life is over. Their countenance is sad, they may withdraw and some allow themselves to fall into habits of poor personal hygiene. This negative feeling is extremely dangerous:

- It saps our ambition.
- It causes us to look at life through gloomy glasses.
- It robs us of our natural energy.
- It knocks us out of the spiritual race.

At times, life may be hard, but it's certainly not over. In Psalm 31:9-12, the psalmist describes his troubles. He says his eye was consumed with grief, his strength failed him because of his sin and he felt he was forgotten as a dead man. But even in such a low state, he could say, *"O love the Lord all ye his saints: for the Lord preserveth the faithful..."* (Psalm 31:23).

Our God is the God of new beginnings and we must draw from the good within us, *"That the communication of thy faith may become effectual by the acknowledging of every good thing which is in you in Christ Jesus"* (Philemon 6).

When we acknowledge the positive the Lord has placed inside our heart and mind, it makes us continually aware of all the good the Lord has done for us. As we think, we will become. In us there is a God-given ability to wait on the Lord, to overcome hurdles, to study and learn and, if necessary, the power to forgive and forget.

Our outlook reminds us that our God can do anything. As Jesus declares, *"With men it is impossible, but not with God: for with God all things are possible"* (Mark 10:27).

This means:

- He can provide us with things which are beyond our grasp.
- Nothing we encounter in life is bigger than God.
- If we exercise faith, we have absolutely nothing to worry about.
- He is the Master Supplier of all our needs.

In view of this, we must keep a positive outlook because it affects our present actions, and our present actions affect our future outcomes. Our time will come!

WAITING ON THE LORD

Still in prison, Joseph maintained the right attitude. Even when things were bleak, he realized his life was not over.

Undoubtedly, he experienced a broad range of emotions. In the early weeks after the butler's release, he probably felt a high level of excitement, which gradually faded. He was disappointed, but he forgave the butler and patiently waited on the Lord.

Joseph knew that no one could ruin God's plans, not his brothers, Potiphar, the jailor, the butler—no one. With the psalmist, he could say, *My soul, wait thou only upon God; for my expectation is from him"* (Psalm 62:5). *"Wait on the Lord; be strong and of good courage, and he shall strengthen thine heart: wait, I say, on the Lord"* (Psalm. 27:14).

DIVINE INTERVENTION

The chief butler had forgotten Joseph, but the Lord had a plan that would jog his memory. Two years after the butler's release, Pharaoh had two dreams. In the first one, he saw seven healthy cows come up out of the river to feed in a meadow. He then saw seven unhealthy cows come up out of the same river. The unhealthy animals ate up the healthy ones. Pharaoh then awakened.

In the second dream, he witnessed seven good ears of corn upon a stalk. He then saw seven thin ears of corn which devoured the good ears.

When Pharaoh woke up, he was troubled in his spirit. He called for all of the magicians and wise men of Egypt and told them his dreams, but they could not interpret them for him.

At this point God intervened. He rendered the ability of the magicians and wise men ineffective.

When God intervenes:

- He performs miracles and does the impossible.
- He will work for us while we are yet in our difficulty.

- He will cause employers to see our true value.
- He will provide finances from unexpected sources.
- He will orchestrate the present so the future will contain promise fulfillment.
- He will mold and equip us to move to our predestined places.
- He will use our gifts and abilities to bring favorable resolution.

God never forgets us and will always come to our rescue. He is the Omniscient One who knows all things.

COWS, CORN AND A FAMINE

Joseph had been faithful through all he had encountered. He was certainly not a crybaby who murmured and complained:

- He endured the rejection and betrayal of his brothers.
- He endured being thrown in and removed from the pit.
- He endured being sold into slavery.
- He endured and overcame the temptation of Potiphar's wife.
- He endured the period of time he had spent in prison, and was now positioned for advancement.

When none of the magicians or wise men could interpret the dreams of Pharaoh, the chief butler said, "I do remember my faults this day." He then went on to tell the king about the interpretations of his and the baker's dreams by Joseph. Immediately, Pharaoh sent to have this man brought to him.

What a moment that must have been for Joseph. It was truly a major shift in his life. The Bible records how that day they hastily brought him out of the dungeon (Genesis 41:14).

After we have stood the test, remained faithful and have been prepared, God will quickly begin our promotion. Joseph had sought earlier to reach Pharaoh, to no avail. Now the tables were turned and Pharaoh was seeking him! He had tried in vain to gain his freedom, and now Pharaoh was ordering his servants to deliver Joseph to him.

He had been in need of clean clothes, a shave and a good bath. Now the king ordered these things be done to make Joseph presentable before him.

Whatever you are facing, be assured the Lord, at the appointed time, will bring you through. He will give you everything He has prepared for you to receive.

Joseph was presented before Pharaoh, who informed him he had been told he could interpret dreams. Joseph said, "It is not in me: God shall give Pharaoh an answer of peace." He gave the glory, honor, and credit to the Lord.

Pharaoh repeated his dreams to Joseph and he interpreted them. He explained to the king that both of his dreams made reference to the same thing. The seven good cows and the seven good ears of corn represented seven years of plenty in Egypt. The seven unhealthy cows and seven thin ears of corn meant seven years of famine.

In summary, Joseph informed him Egypt would experience seven years of abundance followed by seven years of want. The famine was going to be extremely devastating, so the dream was shown twice to Pharaoh to demonstrate this point. He told the king God would soon bring these things to pass—and gave him instructions.

FROM PRISON TO THE PALACE

What a transformation. One minute Joseph was in prison, the next he was telling Pharaoh what to do!

Joseph told the king to find a discreet and wise man and set him over the land of Egypt. He was to let that person appoint officers over the nation to take up the fifth part of the land in the seven years of plenty. They were to gather and store food during the years of abundance for use during the impending years of famine.

Pharaoh and his servants believed the interpretation was accurate, so he told Joseph that since God had shown him the meaning of the dreams, no one else was as wise and discreet as he was. He then declared that all of the people of Egypt would be ruled by Joseph's word, and he alone would be greater than Joseph.

An upward momentum was taking place in Joseph's life. He had been down, yet not defeated. When such a moment arrives:

- The chains of long-term suffering are broken.
- The burdens of oppression are lifted.
- The hardships of the past are removed.
- The preparation for the next level has been completed.
- The powers of oppression cannot hinder or stop us.
- The garments of where we have been are replaced by the garments of where we are going.
- The enemy realizes our victory and their defeat.
- The praise and worship shifts from the struggle to the victory.

By the time Joseph was promoted, he had been in the Egyptian culture long enough to know it well. He had learned to govern and lead in Potiphar's house. Undoubtedly, he had discovered a great deal about the Egyptian government and political structure. He knew how to relate to all types of people, even prisoners. Also, Joseph had strengthened his integrity and his ability to respect leadership—and had managed to wait on the Lord for his "due season."

A TIME TO REAP

As believers we are busily engaged in the work of the Lord, but are challenged by waiting periods. Then there are times we are busy with spiritual labor for extended periods and it seems that our harvest will never come. Though we don't do God's work for material gain, we do expect to see some benefits from our labor.

We need to remember there is always a time period between sowing and reaping, but as Paul writes, *"And let us not be weary in well doing: for in due season we shall reap, if we faint not"* (Galatians 6:9).

In the work of God's Kingdom, the activities we are involved in constitute our "well doing." These may include preaching, teaching, pastoring, evangelizing, outreaching, fasting, praying, Bible study, witnessing and counseling. In all these endeavors we are actually sowing seeds—investing in the Kingdom and laying up treasures in heaven.

In the process we are not to allow our patience, tolerance and pleasure to become so exhausted it affects our ability to function for the Lord. Weariness promotes fainting:

- It is *physical* exhaustion to a level we become drained of our natural energy.
- It is *patience* exhaustion to the extent we are no longer calm in bearing the pains and trials we experience.
- It is *tolerance* exhaustion, or the lack of ability to allow variance from the expected or desired standard.
- It is *pleasure* exhaustion, or the loss of ability to experience delight, joy and desire.

Joseph evidently knew his day of blessing was on the way. He had an unusual ability to handle stressful situations which can cause weariness, yet did not allow this to be a constant state in his life, and he did not faint. His day of reaping had begun and God was using him to interpret the dreams of Pharaoh.

REACHING THE PINNACLE

It was a new day for this Jew in the land of Egypt. *"And Pharaoh said unto Joseph, See I have set thee over all the land of Egypt. And Pharaoh took off his ring from his hand, and put it upon Joseph's hand, and arrayed him in vestures of fine linen, and put a gold chain about his neck; And he made him to ride in the second chariot which he had; and they cried before him, Bow the knee: and he made him ruler over all the land of Egypt. And Pharaoh said unto Joseph, I am Pharaoh, and without thee shall no man lift up his hand or foot in all the land of Egypt. And Pharaoh called Joseph's name Zaphnathpaaneah; and he gave him to wife Asenath the daughter of Potipherah priest of On. And Joseph went out over all the land of Egypt"* (Genesis 41:41-45).

The pinnacle is the highest point of development and achievement. His appointment to the high position he received was certainly not the usual. He was not an Egyptian and had not been raised in their culture as a child. Truly the Lord had His hand upon Joseph.

The fact of the matter is that Pharaoh did not set Joseph over all of Egypt. He was simply the person the Lord used to elevate him. Other individuals sometimes feel they are responsible for our promotions, but in actuality God is in charge.

The honor bestowed on Joseph was earned during his time of suffering:

- He earned the position.
- He earned the ring.
- He earned the fine linen and gold chain.
- He earned the privilege of riding in the second chariot.
- He earned the ability to have the Egyptians bow before him.

All of this was a part of his reward from the Lord for standing in the face of every challenge and passing every test. As the righteous of God, we are the recipients of numerous blessings.

First: Our little is blessed.

"A little that a righteous man hath is better than the riches of many wicked" (Psalm 37:16). This is true because we achieve what we have according to God's guidelines. We use what we possess in a manner the Lord directs. Also, we can use the little we have to lay up treasures in heaven.

Second: We are upheld by the Lord.

"For the arm of the wicked shall be broken: but the Lord upholdeth the righteous" (Psalm 37:17). The Lord lifts and sustains us. Our strength is not of ourselves, but is in the faithful and strong hand of the Lord. We are upheld, like Peter, upon the sinking billows of life. He protects us by being our life foundation, by promoting our interests and by providing for our livelihood.

Third: We are never forsaken.

"I have been young, and now am old; yet have I not seen the

97

righteous forsaken, not his seed begging bread" (Psalm 37:25). The testimony of the psalmist is both precious and encouraging. He speaks about his observances from his youth to his old age. His words testifiy of the reliability and faithfulness of a loving God.

Joseph's little was made much. He was upheld by the Lord, and never forsaken by Him. He was one of God's righteous servants.

He lived before the incarnation of Christ, but as we briefly mentioned earlier, he was a type of Christ:

- He was loved by his father, as Jesus was loved by God, the Father.
- Joseph's father clothed him in a coat of many colors. Jesus' Father clothed Him in the likeness of sinful flesh.
- Joseph's own brothers hated him. Jesus came to a nation of his brethren and many of them despised Him.
- Joseph's brothers rejected him. Jesus' brothers and those in his nation rejected Him.
- They conspired against Joseph as they conspired against Jesus.
- Joseph and Jesus were abused.
- Joseph suffered and he was shamed. Jesus also suffered and He was shamed.
- Joseph's brothers betrayed him for twenty pieces of silver. Jesus was betrayed for thirty pieces of silver.
- Joseph was falsely accused and thrown into captivity. Jesus was falsely accused and thrown into captivity.
- When Joseph was in prison, he interacted with two other prisoners. When Jesus was on the cross, He conversed with two prisoners, and when He was crucified, hung between them.

Joseph was Christ-like and holy, loving, forgiving, patient, durable in suffering, caring and concerned, focused, and full of faith.

REMEMBER WHERE YOU CAME FROM

When Joseph reached the pinnacle, he remembered where he came from. He had gone through so much that he could not forget how far the Lord had brought him. He had risen from the darkness of the pit and was now enjoying the light of success.

Moses also remembered his roots. In his parting address in Deuteronomy 31:4, he spoke of how the Lord destroyed Sihon and Og, kings of the Amorites. Joshua, in his farewell words, recounted much of what the Lord had done, telling major facts concerning Israel's history, along with God's involvement. At the time of their parting, they were still reminiscing how far the Lord had brought them.

It is important to remember our progress:

1. It promotes our appreciation of the Lord.

When we look back over our lives and consider the significance of God's intervention, we soon come to realize we could not have reached our current destination without Him. Our life promotions have taken place because He personally brought them to pass.

2. It reminds us of our inability to come so far on our own.

Some of us had such humble beginnings that success seemed to be painfully out of reach. The Lord's enhancement and blessings upon our lives lifted us above our inability and brought success.

3. It promotes our humility.

When we achieve, with God's help, what we could not have realized on our own, we are humbled before Him and others.

4. It enables us to properly relate to those who are still where we came from.

The Lord's concern is we reach levels which will enable us to be used by Him to be a blessing to others. When we move from where we were and are promoted, we gain the knowledge of the process involved. The sharing of this with persons who are where we *were* is key to their promotion and elevation.

5. It keeps us from becoming untouchable or unreachable.

If we are humbled by what the Lord has done for us, we will posture ourselves in a manner that others can reach us and receive benefit from our lives through our counsel to them.

6. It can resist pride and arrogance.

We have no basis to become egotistical. Our achievements, whatever they are, have been brought by the Lord. Since we could not have made it without Him, we have no reason to become filled with false pride or arrogance.

Because Joseph remembered where he came from, I believe he could handle the pinnacle. The road he had traveled had strengthened his relationship with the Lord. It made him resilient in the face of opposition. It built his resistance to sin and his resolution to patiently endure hardship.

THE VALUE OF THE ANOINTING

The Lord preordained Joseph to receive his assignment in Egypt—and gave him the power for its accomplishment. Joseph was anointed and was empowered to fulfill his calling.

Our anointing—directed godly power—is from the Lord to perform His purposes. The Lord God is the Omnipotent One. He alone is Creator, Sustainer and Governor.

Jesus Christ is "The Anointed One," and His anointing flows from Him, the Head, down to those of us who comprise His body. Godly power is needed to overthrow demonic powers, to remove enemy strongholds and to carry on kingdom business in the face of enemy opposition. *"And it shall come to pass in that day, that his burden shall be taken from off thy shoulder, and his yoke from off thy neck, and the yoke shall be destroyed because of the anointing"* (Isaiah 10:27).

It is distributed according to God's will and He alone determines who receives which type of anointing—given to those who are His redeemed ones (Ephesians 1:7). His distribution is not based upon the work we do, the positions we occupy, the money we have or our family ties. Joseph was not selected because he was born into a good family. He was chosen before he or his relatives came to exist in the earth.

The anointing will set us apart. It is quite clear Joseph was ordained to be removed from his family. I am sure he didn't understand much of what was happening to him, but he handled it well.

Those who are anointed know that godly separation from others can promote godly focus. They realize that time away from others can be used as moments to spend with the Lord. They know that separation time is *preparation* time for our upward climb to the pinnacle. They discover that being set apart is a means of advancing toward greater anointing.

With God's touch we will experience a move from the natural to the supernatural. Our operation will be in the Spirit, not the flesh. We will gain spiritual capability beyond our own because when we function in the anointing, the outcome is miraculously different.

The anointing reveals friends and enemies. It is most distressing that the touch of God on Joseph's life caused him so much heartache within his own family. The favor shown him by his father was orchestrated by the Lord because of his anointing.

DETERMINED, NOT DISCOURAGED

The achievement of reaching the summit will not happen without some resistance, but successful people are those who have grown determined in their attitude. Many never achieve what they are capable of because they lack the firm commitment to what they intend to do or bring about.

True determination is affected by our desire. A person dying of thirst, in most cases, will push on in search of water based upon his or her craving—and the will to live. Strong desire causes one to

101

maintain focus and give their all. We will seek every approach to achieve and will work day and night to reach the objective. We will take courses, attend seminars and workshops and will not be detoured by major obstructions or minor trivialities. The lack of needed resources or family support will be overcome.

True determination has durability:

- It has a "will not be stopped" attitude.
- It can take the blow of failure, disappointment and opposition.
- It can undergo hardship and keep moving forward.
- It has the same effect upon discouragement that light has upon darkness.
- In the face of defeat, it drives with the same force as it does when all is going well.
- By it, victories are achieved that could easily have been losses.
- It takes discouragement by the collar, looks it straight in the eyes and says, "there is no room for you in this circumstance."

When situations are critical and there seems to be no help, many will panic. They will experience sudden overwhelming fright—an unreasoning terror. When it strikes many act out of fear rather than faith. They do things which make matters worse, not thinking clearly or logically.

The doorway to our thoughts must always be guarded since our thinking will either come under the authority of the Holy Spirit or our carnal man. The enemy wants to fill our minds with the negative and bring weakness. He desires to cause us to become confused, troubled, and to eventually break down. On the other hand, the Holy Spirit longs to strengthen our minds and bring peace.

Joseph's determination did not allow room for discouragement to take control of his thinking.

THE TIME OF PROMOTION

We do not want to expend time, energy, money and more without receiving some sort of benefit. It's a sign our efforts are fruitful.

Promotions, however, are based upon performance. As we engage in our callings, our work is actually being rated and evaluated. During the entire time of Joseph's testing, his performance was being examined. The Lord tries us to let us see where we stand and the extent to which we have grown. It's much like taking exams to move from one year of college to the next.

In God's Kingdom, if we want spiritual promotions, we must perform spiritual activities and pass spiritual tests at the level specified by the Lord. *"For promotion cometh neither from the east, nor from the west, nor from the south"* (Psalm 75:6). The north is probably not mentioned because it is sometimes associated with God's dwelling place (Isaiah 14:13; Psalm 48:2). The north signifies the secret place, and from the secret of God's counsel promotion comes.

Remember, He is infinitely wise and powerful, and has the authority to set up and put down as He chooses.

Thankfully, the Lord desires our happiness and promotion. *"And all things, whatsoever ye shall ask in prayer, believing, ye shall receive"* (Matthew 21:22). *"Ask, and it shall be given you; seek and ye shall find; knock, and it shall be opened unto you"* (Matthew 7:7).

Scripture is filled with proof God desires our well being and advancement. His Word is a guide and, if followed, will bring our promotion.

When we walk with the Lord, He will orchestrate our lives in ways which lift us higher. Job suffered and lost everything, yet in the end he was advanced beyond his previous level.

The Lord knew exactly what it would take to prepare Joseph for his assignment, and all of the required ingredients were a part of His divine orchestration.

IN CHARGE!

God's timing is such that when we reach the pinnacle, we will be ready to operate there.

The Lord prepared Joseph. He was experienced, competent, and blessed. Pharaoh took his ring and put it upon Joseph's hand. He gave

Asenath to Joseph for his wife.

They had two sons, Manasseh (God hath made me forget all my toil, and all my father's house), and Ephraim (God hath caused me to be fruitful in the land of my affliction). Their names depicted his life.

Joseph wisely stored food during the seven years of plenty. He gathered corn as the sand of the sea until he stopped numbering. When the famine came, Pharaoh sent all the needy to Joseph. In fact, people from many parched nations sent representatives to purchase grain and supplies.

FULFILLING THE DREAM

Jacob, Joseph's father, heard there was corn in Egypt and sent Joseph's brothers there to buy what was needed. All of the brothers went except Benjamin (He and Joseph had the same mother).

When they arrived in Egypt, Joseph was governor and they came and bowed down before him—fulfilling the earlier dream. Joseph knew them, but they did not recognize him. He tested his brothers, treating them harshly, and charged them as spies.

They denied the accusation and told Joseph they had journeyed for food and were all the sons of one man. They also informed him that another brother was at home, and that one brother was dead—referring to Joseph whom they *assumed* was dead.

To further test their word, Joseph said that one of the men had to go home and return with the younger brother. He informed them he was going to keep one of them with him in Egypt until they returned.

The siblings remembered their sin and confessed their guilt before God. Joseph understood them, but they did not know it because he spoke to them via an interpreter.

At a subsequent meeting, Joseph revealed to his brothers he was the brother whom they had sold into slavery. Convinced of their repentance, he forgave and blessed them—not wanting his brothers to be grieved or angry with themselves for their deed.

He stated that God had sent him before them to preserve their lives. He fell upon his brother Benjamin's neck and kissed him and embraced all of his brothers and they wept and talked.

FORGIVENESS BRINGS THE BLESSING

The brothers returned home and told their father Joseph was alive and was the governor over all the land of Egypt. Jacob's heart fainted, for he could hardly believe his ears!

God told Jacob not to fear going down to Egypt because He would make a great nation of him. Jacob went to the land of Pharaoh with all of his family (Genesis 46:27) where Joseph gave them a portion of land. They had possessions and grew and multiplied exceedingly (Genesis 47:27).

Joseph had come this far, but would have harmed his success if he had not forgiven his brothers. When we forgive, we keep ourselves positioned to be favored of the Lord. Forgiveness keeps the channel of blessings open.

Like Joseph, success can be yours if you hold fast to your dreams and visions. Believe in God and yourself, properly utilize your time and energy, face and conquer difficult challenges and constantly celebrate the achievements God has blessed you to make.

Be willing to do what the Lord says, even if some call you foolish. Be aware of the extent of your resources and remain seriously committed to God's cause and purpose for your life.

Once more, the Lord is saying, "You can do it!"

CHAPTER 4

FAITH THAT FIGHTS

A ccording to an old proverb, "When a man has liberty to go into the treasure house of a king to enrich himself, he must first seek the keys to open the door."

Likewise, if we desire to be favored with God's grace we must have faith—which is the only key to the Father's abundance."

What is faith?" According to the Word, it is *"...the substance of things hoped for, the evidence of things not seen"* (Hebrews 11:1). This "substance" gives us assurance, freedom from doubt and inspires confidence. Plus the fact we have "evidence" demands acceptance of its truth—the guarantee we will have what we do not see.

It is belief in action. As Martin Luther once said, "Our faith is a lively, reckless, confidence in God."

THE CORNERSTONES

Before we can see tangible results, a foundation must be built for belief and expectation. There are six cornerstones:

First: We must know the God of our faith.

The first four words in the Bible say it all: *"In the beginning God..."* (Genesis 1:1). This is the basis of all we believe—the bedrock of our existence. Knowing the Almighty said "Let there be" and created everything we know is basic to our faith.

He is to be praised as Creator, trusted as Sovereign Lord and worshiped as Eternal God. He alone has the power to redeem, renew, and recreate. He is Provident—governing the world. And His works are holy, wise and powerful. *"The Lord by wisdom hath founded the earth; by understanding hath he established the heavens"* (Proverbs 3:19).

Our Omnipotent (all-powerful), Omniscient (all-knowing), Omnipresent (all-present) God has no limitations and is bounded only by His own nature and will. This is all we need to have ultimate faith in Him.

Second: We must know we can depend on God.

The Lord's faithfulness refers to His loyalty to Himself and His entire creation. He will not change His character or fail to perform all that He has promised. *"God is faithful, by whom ye were called unto the fellowship of his Son Jesus Christ our Lord"* (1 Corinthians 1:9). *"God is faithful when we encounter temptation"* (1 Corinthians 10:13). *"Faithful is he that calleth you, who also will do it"* (1 Thessalonians 5:24). *"But the Lord is faithful, who shall stablish you, and keep you from evil"* (2 Thesssalonians 3:3).

Third: We must understand the faith process.

The Creator is One of order and procedure. *"So then faith cometh by hearing, and hearing by the word of God"* (Romans 10:17). Also involved in the process is mental agreement. We must *agree* that what we hear in the Word is true—and strong enough to transform our lives.

Fourth: There must be commitment to the truth.

When faith is mentioned in the New Testament, it speaks of personal commitment to what is genuine and valid. A man or woman of faith hears the truth, agrees with it, and then takes action.

Fifth: We must have the "God kind" of faith.

The Almighty sees the invisible as reality—and so must we. Faith provides the connection to what is real. It sees the victory before it takes place, eradicates fear and doubt, occupies the mind with favorable outcomes and brings promotion, not demotion. Faith also provides mental pictures of the result we are believing for and causes us to step out when we would not normally do so.

Sixth: We must know the object of our faith.

Where is your faith directed? There can only be one answer—and it is found in the words of Jesus when He declared, "Have faith in God" (Mark 11:22). He is the One who cannot lie, who cannot change, who cannot fail.

GROUNDED, EXERCISED AND ENCOURAGED

As a pastor, I've been asked, "What is the best way for faith to operate in my life?"

Let me offer these three suggestions:

Our faith must be properly grounded.

"Being born again, not of corruptible seed, but of incorruptible, by the word of God, which liveth and abideth for ever" (1 Peter 1:23).

The foundation of our faith is the basis upon which our belief and actions are established. Our "ground" is the Word, which is not only pure, but sure. Scripture declares, *"...the word of our God shall stand forever"* (Isaiah 40:8). *"Forever, O Lord, thy word is settled in heaven"* (Psalm 119:89). The *ground* of our faith—the Word—is as faithful as the Object of our faith—Jesus.

Our faith must be properly exercised.

Abraham believed God and left his home, not knowing where he was going. He had a Word from the Lord. Caleb believed God when he said, *"Let us go up at once and possess it"* (Numbers 13:30). God promised him land, and he believed even though the difficulties were great and seemed numberless. Peter exercised his faith when he said, *"Nevertheless, at thy word I will let down the net"* (Luke 5:5).

Our faith must be properly encouraged.

Joshua inspired and stimulated his faith when he said, *"There failed not ought of any good thing which the Lord had spoken unto the house of Israel; all came to pass"* (Joshua 21:45). Solomon's testimony was, *"Blessed be the Lord, there hath not failed one word of all which he promised"* (1 Kings 8:56). In Mark 14:13-16, Jesus told the disciples about a man with a pitcher of water who would lead them to the master of the house to provide a place for the Passover. If they had not obeyed, they would not have experienced the truthfulness of His Word.

True faith should be encouraged—and true faith encourages us!

MUSTARD SEED FAITH

A poor widow was weeping in the room where the body of her husband was laying after death. Their only child came in, and said, "Why do you weep so, mother?"

The mother told him of the father's death and referred to their poverty. Looking into her face, the little boy said, "Is God dead, mother?"

So many times believers let their life activities affect them as though the Almighty is no longer alive. Situations might not be as we would wish, but God is still on the throne—watching over the affairs of man.

Even the smallest amount of belief can work wonders. Jesus said, *"If ye have faith as a grain of a mustard seed....nothing shall be impossible unto you"* (Matthew 17:20).

It is unnecessary to itemize all of the possibilities of our faith since it is written, *"According to your faith, be it unto you"* (Matthew 9:29). There is no limit: if you can believe, *all* things are possible (Mark 9:23).

The noted English preacher, Charles Spurgeon, observed, "Our faith is the center of the target at which God doth shoot when He tries us; and if any other grace shall escape untried, certainly faith shall not." Whatever our level of faith, we will be tried.

THE FOLLY OF UNBELIEF

When God looks at the heart, He knows how much or how little faith is present. In some cases there is *none!*

During the great exodus from Egypt, it was the unbelief of many Israelites that kept them from entering and seeing the Promised Land (Hebrews 3:19). Even in Christ's day, the lack of belief among the

Nazarenes prevented them from witnessing His miracles (Matthew 13:58).

Unbelief dishonors God. When Eve believed the serpent, she demonstrated her disrespect for the Creator who placed her in the garden. And it was unbelief that drove the nails into the hands and feet of Jesus, pierced His heart, brought His suffering and death and still produces sin and sorrow.

It is folly to presume you can succeed without God.

THE FAILURE OF UNBELIEF

Moses sent twelve men to spy out the land of Canaan, yet only Caleb and Joshua returned with a favorable report. The other ten men acted with scepticism and measured the difficulty in terms of human strength. As a result, they stated the people of Canaan were stronger than the Israelites and the people were of great stature: "They were as giants and we were as grasshoppers before them."

The problem resulted from giving priority to the flesh instead of to the power of God.

A major reason this fails is because it makes the Word of God appear void. The spies told Moses the land consumed its inhabitants. Yet God had already told them that it was a bountiful, large land that flowed with milk and honey (Exodus 3:8).

Unbelief contradicts God because it can only judge by appearance. If He had already informed them of the blessings of Canaan, why should they doubt?

If we fail to believe we will be shut out from the favor and abundance of the Almighty.

THE TRIUMPH OF FAITH

Thank God our faith does not have to result in folly or failure. It can be victorious. Let me tell you why:

Faith confirms the promises of God. Scripture contains a wealth of pledges, vows and covenants made by the Lord. These promises are given to believers, yet we must exercise faith to receive fulfillment of

111

them. That's how we see them become reality.

It's been said His promises are an inexhaustible mine of wealth, an arsenal containing all manner of offensive and defensive weapons, they are surgery and ointment for wounds, peace in confusion and calm in anxiety. They comprise a highway of golden promises which leads from the depths of degradation all the way to the Father's house.

Faith exhibits proof of God's faithfulness.

The Bible records how the spies brought back succulent fruit from Canaan and showed it to Moses and Aaron (Numbers 13:26). The Lord told them of the abundance of the land, but his faithfulness became tangible when they acquired the fruit.

- By faith they were able to bring into the wilderness what the wilderness could not produce.
- By faith we can bring into our situations what our situations cannot produce.
- By faith our lives are to manifest in the world what the world cannot produce.

Many believers speak of God's faithfulness, yet what they experience is far below what is possible with strong belief and expectation.

Faith advocates present possession.

Caleb said, "Let us go up at once and possess it." If God has made us a promise, we should believe Him and step out immediately—not waiting for a more convenient time. Faith values the present because it knows our future harvests depend on our current actions. If you need a fresh anointing, a healing, a friend, a financial breakthrough, burdens removed, yokes destroyed, family unity or a career boost, faith says it is yours right now.

Faith grieves at the folly of unbelief.

When the ten spies returned with their negative report, saying they could not defeat the enemy, the people became extremely upset (Numbers 14:1). They not only wept and cried that night, they murmured against Moses and Aaron. Joshua and Caleb had such grief and regret over the fearful reports that they tore their clothes.

It grieves people of faith to see others operating in unbelief. Only those who truly trust God can know the foolishness and sin of doubting.

Faith rests totally in the Lord.
Joshua and Caleb declared, *"If the Lord delight in us, then he will bring us into this land, and give it us; a land which flows with milk and honey"* (v.8). They spoke the same words of promise the Lord had given to Moses.

Faith does not overlook life's difficulties, but knows the problems cannot compare to the power of God. Unbelief *excludes* the Lord in its process, while faith says "nothing is too hard for God."

When we rest in the Lord we do not allow ourselves to become so focused on negative situations that we lose hope. We simply accept His promises by faith and leave the rest to Him.

Faith follows God always and everywhere.
Scripture records that Caleb followed the Lord *"fully"* (v.24). As a result, he was allowed to enter into Canaan with Joshua when others of their generation perished in the wilderness. Caleb stayed close to the Lord and was a firm believer in promise fulfillment.

The number of giants or the obstacles ahead do not matter. Faith keeps us connected with the Lord and allows us to follow Him—wherever He may lead.

Faith inherits God's promises.
The Lord said of Caleb, *"...him will I bring into the land"* (v.24).

When faith is present, it latches onto God's promises and refuses to release them. It has a delivery record that is superior to the U.S. Postal Service, UPS and Federal Express combined. It knows if God makes a promise, He will fulfill it—and that His fulfillment cannot be stopped or altered.

Those of us who will go to heaven must have our own faith. In Gideon's camp, every soldier had his own pitcher. Among Solomon's men of valor, everyone wore his own sword, and all of these

113

experienced victory.

Only the five wise virgins who had oil in their lamps could enter in with the bridegroom. If we are to inherit the Father's promises, we must do it God's way.

THE OPERATION OF EFFECTIVE FAITH

There's a vast difference between human hope and spiritual expectation. When we exercise our belief according to God's Laws our faith becomes effective.

What we are discussing is faith in the Lord Jesus that depends on Him. It is strengthened under pressure and causes us to face situations with anticipation instead of dread. It believes in God's character, promises, and in His power to perform.

The shipwreck of apostle Paul shows the power of effective faith (Acts 27). When King Agrippa came to Caesarea to salute Festus, the new governor, he was told the story of Paul, the prisoner. Agrippa was informed that the charges brought against Paul had not been proven, and that the follower of Christ had appealed to Caesar.

Festus hoped Agrippa would help him out of the unfair predicament of sending a prisoner to Augustus without being able to list the crimes against him. When Paul was brought out to speak, he spoke of his conversion to Christ. This so affected Festus that he thought Paul had gone mad. Agrippa, too, was so touched he said, *"Almost thou persuadest me to be a Christian."*

By faith, Paul became a changed, empowered, obedient, divinely helped, devoted, faithful and satisfied man. His trip to Rome reveals much about effective faith.

From this story we discover:

Our faith is effective in all situations.

As the ship which carried Paul was sailing to Italy, a wind arose and the apostle told the passengers and crew that their voyage would include much harm and damage to the ship—and to their lives. However, the centurion believed the "good report" of the master and owner of the ship and they continued after the south wind calmed.

Shortly thereafter, a storm arose and before long the ship and all

YOU CAN DO IT!

aboard were endangered. The seas were so violent they had to throw much of the contents of the hold overboard. Paul told them if they had listened to him they would not have suffered loss or been in danger.

Paul's "faith situation" was perilous—one that exposed him to injury and death. However, effective faith works in all circumstances, no matter how severe. It operates in times which are good and bad, wealthy and poor, high and low—the best and worst times.

Our faith reassures us of God's backing.

The apostle declared, "No man will lose his life, but we'll lose the ship." He further said that the angel of God whom he belonged to and served told him he should not fear because he had to be brought before Caesar. He also proclaimed that the Lord would spare all who sailed with him.

Effective faith focuses upon the promises of God and recalls them when needed for strength. It allows us to simply accept His Word and step into the unknown. This assures us of His presence and enables us to accept what He allows.

Our faith gives birth to faithful proclamations.

Paul said, "Be of good cheer, for I believe God, that it shall be as it was told me." His proclamation was based on what he felt inwardly. The Lord allowed him to experience cheer so he could encourage others—even during a life-threatening event.

When our faith is effective, we see what it sees, speak what it speaks, do what it says to do, and act as it says we are to act.

Paul's focus was upon the Word of the Lord, not upon the danger of his situation. He proclaimed that all would be well. Since the angel told him everyone on board would survive, the apostle knew he could not die until God's purpose for him was fulfilled.

The same thing can be said about us. We cannot depart from this place because the Lord's plan for us is not complete. Instead of complaining over our present difficulties, we must declare our blessings.

Our faith has conditions that must be met.

Paul announced, "Except ye abide in the ship, ye cannot be saved." He warned that if the sailors were allowed to desert the vessel, they would drown. You see, the promise had a condition—they must stay with the ship!

- In 1 John 3:22, we have the promise we will receive whatsoever we ask of Him. The condition is that we do His commandments.
- In Matthew 6:33, the promise is that all things will be added to us. The condition is we seek God's Kingdom first.
- In Joshua 1:8, God promised that Joshua's way would be prosperous and he would have good success. The condition was that he would obey God's law.
- In Mark 11:23, the promise is that the things we say shall come to pass. The condition is we do not doubt but believe what we say shall come to pass.
- In Matthew 21:22, the promise is we will receive all things we ask in prayer. The condition is that we believe.

It is comforting to know that all conditions are met when we abide in the Word.

Our faith has transforming power.

As we read Acts 27:29, all of their hope was gone, but in verse 36 they were of good cheer. The apostle told his shipmates to take meat and eat, because not one hair would fall from the head of any of them. He reassured them they would all be safe.

Paul's faith was spoken and manifested to such a degree that it brought joy to the others. Effective faith turns panic into calm, anxiety into peace, despair into hope, sorrow into happiness, defeat into victory and lack into plenty. It will transform us in the midst of our tribulation.

Our faith produces victory.

The men had a frightening time at sea, yet despite all of their concerns, they made it safely to dry land. Paul was on board and all on the ship were blessed because of his presence. Faith in God results in triumph. Long ago, someone penned these words:

Faith is the foot of the soul—so it comes to Christ.
Faith is the hand of the soul—so it receives Christ.
Faith is the arm of the soul—so it embraces Christ.
Faith is the eye of the soul—so it looks to Christ.
Faith is the mouth of the soul—so it feeds on Christ.

JOYFUL TRUTHS

What a dreary sad world it would be if God created a universe without hope and a future without positive expectation. Instead, He planted within each of us a certain amount of belief. As Paul writes, *"...God hath dealt to every man the measure of faith"* (Romans 12:3).

Because of this, we have reasons to rejoice.

Faith in God is precious.

Because of its own infinite possibilities, faith must be cherished and treasured. With it, nothing we need is impossible. It is the hand which takes with a firm, unfailing grip, the faithful promises of God. By it we are justified (Romans 5:1), sanctified (Acts 26:18), we live (Romans 1:17), we stand (Romans 11:20), we walk (2 Corinthians 5:70) and we wait (Galatians 5:5).

To trust Him partially is not faith, rather an invitation to fail. Our faith is precious and God glorifies it because it glorifies Him.

Faith in God is progressive.

Paul commended the Thessalonians because their faith grew exceedingly. Faith will flourish where there is a growing awareness and communion with God-like love, it does not have to be forced or driven, it simply must be fed and inspired. We must progress from merely confessing faith to actually *living* faith.

117

Our faith in God is related to our knowledge of Him.
We can never be redeemed through a second-hand experience. Knowledge of the Lord comes through our personal association with Him.

- The testimony of another person encourages me, but my own testimony empowers me.
- What I understand about the Lord from another person is how they perceive Him to be, but what I know about Him myself is how I *know* Him to be.
- What another believer tells me about Him will help me *in* a storm, but what I experience myself will get me *through* the storm.

PRESSING THROUGH

Let me tell you about a man named Jairus.

He was a ruler of the synagogue, a chief official and prominent member of his community—and he believed in God.

During a time when his daughter was sick to the point of death, Jairus sought out Jesus. He pressed through the crowd, humbled himself and fell at the Lord's feet.

Only those who truly believe will put forth the effort to demonstrate their faith and touch Jesus.

- We must press through negativity which says we won't make it to the Lord.
- We must press through doubt which says Jesus will not act on our behalf.
- We must press through discouragement, which says there is no sense in going on.
- We must press beyond overwhelming circumstances that say we have already lost.
- We must press through fear which says this problem or situation will either destroy or permanently damage us.
- We must press through past mistakes, which say this will be another failure.

FORTY-SIX ATTRIBUTES OF PEOPLE OF FAITH

In the story of Jairus—and other men and women in God's Word—we find character attributes which distinguish people of faith. As you study this list, ask yourself, "Is this me? Do I possess this quality?"

If not, spend whatever time it takes for the Lord to fill your heart, soul and mind with the faith and belief only He can give.

1. People of faith boldly make their requests to Jesus.

After pressing through the throng to reach the Master, Jairus presented his situation, telling Him that his daughter was sick and at the point of death (Luke 8). He dreaded the thought and feared she would die at any moment.

Have you ever been at a breaking point? It's an uncomfortable position to be in.

Jairus urgently requested that Jesus go with him to his house and lay His hands on her, believing if He did so, His daughter would be healed and live. Even though he didn't fully understand, he knew that when Jesus laid His hand on individuals, the blind saw, the sick were healed and the lame walked.

2. People of faith will get a response from the Lord.

In that crowd, Jesus singled out this man and followed Jairus to his home. Why? Because the Lord saw a person of faith.

His fellow religious rulers were violently opposed to Jesus, and they voiced their opinions publicly. Jairus ran the risk of their hostility and of being censored by them.

The demeanor of this man was one of humility, falling at His feet, laying aside all pride. His approach was both pleading and expectant, fully believing his daughter would be raised.

3. People of faith can endure delay.

As Jesus moved through the crowd with Jairus, a woman with an

119

issue of blood called after Him. She was desperate for a miracle, and when she touched Jesus' garment by faith, she was healed.

While the Lord was talking to the woman, certain persons came from Jairus' house and told him not to trouble Jesus anymore because his daughter had died. At this point, Jairus could have walked away, but he didn't. He seemed to take the situation as a delay and not a denial.

On one hand, Jairus was told his daughter was dead and it was over. On the other hand, Jesus told him not to fear, but to believe.

We must learn to endure the delays that sometimes occur during our periods of waiting upon the Lord. Whatever the length of the wait, we will be more than rewarded when our expectations are fulfilled.

4. People of faith will receive.

When Jesus arrived with Jairus at his house there was a crowd already gathered—and a great noise arose from the mourners. Jesus inquired concerning all the fuss that was going on, then told them the girl was not dead, just asleep.

Jesus told the mourners to leave, but allowed the father, mother, Peter, James, and John to go with Him to the child. Jesus commanded the girl to arise and immediately she came out of the bed and walked. They were all astonished.

I encourage you to trust God completely. He has spoken concerning what He is going to do and His word shall not return unto Him void, but will accomplish what He pleases (Isaiah 55:11). His hand is not shortened that He cannot save (Isaiah 59:1). His ear is not heavy that He cannot hear (v.1). His eyes are upon us (Psalm 34:15). His feet have all things under them (1 Corinthians 15:27). He will not cast us off, neither will He forsake us (Psalm 94:14).

5. People of faith value the word of God.

Jesus was standing by the lake of Gennesaret teaching the Word. As He taught, the people once more pressed in to hear Him. It is vital that we seek to learn and apply the Word. It converts the soul, makes the simple wise, rejoices the heart, enlightens the eyes, strengthens us against sin and endures forever.

Remember, faith comes by hearing and hearing by the Word of

God. The Word is food for the spirit man, providing wisdom, revelation, direction and guidance. Those who grow to strong faith come to understand the value of scripture.

6. People of faith have devoted possessions.
Jesus saw two ships by the lake. The fishermen had come out of them, and were washing their nets. The vessels had been used unsuccessfully, and were now standing unused.

We must not allow our abilities and possessions to lie dormant too long. Our possessions are not only material, but include our gifts, talents and skills.

Jesus went into Peter's boat and requested that he venture out a little farther from the land. The vessel was ready for the Master's use and Jesus sat down and taught the people from the ship.

All that we have must be ready for the Lord's use—our abilities, professional knowledge, experience, finances, and our material possessions. These were given to us by the Lord, and should be used to further His cause.

7. People of faith perform their commissions.
Jesus gave a gracious mission to Peter, telling Him to launch out into the deep and let down his net for a catch. Even though they had toiled all night and caught nothing, Peter obeyed.

We can never have what God has promised if we stubbornly stay where we are, just as Peter could not have caught any fish if he stayed on dry land.

The secret of success in our Christian labor is to be guided by the Lord. We can think of all kinds of reasons why we should not launch out, but we must, because the Lord instructs us to.

8. People of faith honor God with their faith resolutions.
The decisions we make by faith honor the Lord. Peter was exhausted after fishing all night with nothing to show for his efforts. However, he resolved to act by faith:

■ Not by his mind, thinking there were no fish.
■ Not by his experience, having failed to catch any fish.

121

■ Not by his body, being too tired.

We must trust God no matter what obstacles we encounter. Peter said, "Nevertheless at thy word I will let down the net."

Perhaps you have done the best you know how, but you are weary of trying on your own. God will be honored if today you say, "I won't worry; I will trust God. I won't fear; I will trust the Lord. He is fixing it right now."

In Peter's situation, the night had passed, yet Jesus spoke to him in the present. We must not let yesterday hinder today, but make a fresh start on Jesus' authority. The Lord simply told him to do the same thing he had done all night.

We often look for the Lord to tell us to do things differently, but He sometimes tells us to take the same action. Do as He says.

9. People of faith are amazingly satisfied.

Peter and the others returned to the sea, and they caught a multitude of fish—so many their nets began to break. This time they were more successful "out of season" than they were before "in season." They fished during the night because it was the normal time to fish. Jesus had them launch out at an hour they would not have gone under typical conditions. It is not important when or where you fish, but when and where Jesus tells you to. Peter was amazingly satisfied.

10. People of faith are a blessing to others.

When Peter's ship became overloaded, he called the others so they could also fill their boats. We are blessed to bless others and must be willing to share the bounty we receive.

DIVINE INTENTION

At times, I have sat down and considered how many blessings I have missed simply because I lacked the faith to possess them—even abundance the Lord intended for me to receive.

Divine intention is that which God has in mind for us, and is often something human intention wars against:

YOU CAN DO IT!

- By divine intention we have been saved. We are now re-created beings, new creations in Christ, cleansed by His blood.
- By divine intention we have been called. He called us from our former worldly positions to become what He has purposed. We have been called to liberty (Galatians 5:13).
- By divine intention we have been given Kingdom assignments.
- By divine intention we have been uniquely created and endowed with spiritual gifts.
- By divine intention we are now privileged. We have a High Priest who cares for us, forgives our sins, redeems us from destruction, crowns us with loving kindness and satisfies us with good things.
- By divine intention we are commissioned to *perform* our Kingdom assignments.

Even though Peter failed the Lord and denied Him three times, God did not remove His intention for him. Faith in the Lord causes us to know we can rise even after we fail.

11. People of faith will go to Jesus.
We must always be mindful of who we are to seek in every situation. Mark 2:3 says a man with palsy was brought by four other men to Jesus. They believed they could achieve the desired result by being in the presence of the Lord. While we may sometimes try other sources, the ultimate authority on anything or anyone we are dealing with is Jesus. He has the power of infinite provision.

12. People of faith agree in faith.
In the case of the man with palsy, the four men who carried him were united together in faith and belief. When we are petitioning the Lord for answers in life, it is encouraging to have others agree with us in prayer. At times there may be issues we want to keep just between us and God, but more often we need to form a band of believers who will pray "in one accord."

123

13. People of faith are assured that there is a way.

When the four men saw the huge crowd in the house where Jesus was ministering, they could have been discouraged. Yet they were not. It made them more determined than ever to find a way to bring their crippled friend before the Man who could perform miracles. Our certainty and confidence will show in our behavior. True faith will cause us to act in faith, talk faith, and be assured of possession.

14. People of faith are not easily discouraged.

The men who carried the sick man faced a daunting task. The bed was heavy. Undoubtedly they had been scorned by some of the people in the crowd—and were probably tired and sweaty as they worked to assure his safety.

There also came a point when they realized they could not get any closer to the house. However, this wasn't a time to stop, rather to pause. Undeterred, they climbed up on the housetop, pulled back some of the tiles and created an opening.

This should be a lesson for all of us. We have dealt with things long enough and endured many difficulties, yet we can't give up! We are still in the fight of faith, and the Lord is about to bless us beyond measure.

15. People of faith lay their situations before Jesus.

After removing the tiles, they let the man down through the roof—into the very presence of the Lord. In His presence:

A- All is well

B- Bondages are broken

C- Curses are removed

D- Demons flee

E- Edification comes

F- Faith is built

G- Gifts of the Spirit are birthed and strengthened

H- Hope is kept alive

I- Increase comes

J- Joy is made full

K- Knowledge is received

L- Life is received and made abundant
M- Manifold blessings are received
N- Necessities are provided
O- Opposition is overcome
P- Power is received
Q- Questions are answered
R- Restoration comes
S- Supernatural strength is provided
T- Temptation is overcome
U- Understanding comes
V- Victory is assured
W- Worship is best and ways are made perfect.
X- X-ray vision is perfected (the ability to see the unseen things by faith)
Y- Yielding to God is perfected
Z- Zeal in Christ is strengthened.

Lay your need at the feet of Jesus. Talk to Him about your situation—even though He already knows every detail.

16. People of faith overcome.

I would love to have been there when they lowered the sick man through the roof before Jesus. Scripture records, *"When Jesus saw their faith, he said unto the sick of the palsy, Son, thy sins be forgiven thee"* (Mark 2:4).

He said this so the Pharisees would know He has the power upon earth to forgive sins. Then Jesus told the man to arise, take up his bed and go home. The man immediately arose, totally healed—and now he was carrying the bed that had been used to carry him! He was praising God!

17. People of faith give thanks.

As we are exercising faith in the Lord and waiting for the granting of our requests, we should express our thanks for all He has done, is doing, and will do.

We are to give thanks always— and for all things (Ephesians 5:20). It takes faith to do this—especially when thanksgiving does not

125

seem appropriate for some of our situations. Yet we must accept things as they are, in tough times, easy times, in friendship and adversity, in great harvests and small harvests, when we are pleased and when we are displeased, when doors open and when they are shut.

Our thanks to God manifests our thoughtfulness of Him and our obedience to the leading of the Holy Spirit. It is a sign of our maturity when we can be appreciative of Him in every situation.

ATTACKING THE ENEMY

Let me tell you about a man of faith named Jonathan.

The Philistines had mobilized a large army with thousands of chariots and foot soldiers. They had set up a base camp at Micmash, and were poised to attack, capture and oppress the Israelites. Three raiding parties had been sent out by the enemy to harass, plunder and to demoralize Israel (1 Samuel 13:17). Later, a fourth detachment of soldiers had been dispatched to set up an outpost and to guard the pass at Micmash to prevent a surprise attack by Israel.

The Philistines had organized their forces to make certain of Israel's defeat. However, what happened next is one of the most daring, fearless feats by an individual in the annals of military history. We see Jonathan, the son of Saul, willing to step out by faith to achieve a victory for Israel.

18. People of faith love the Lord and His cause.

Jonathan loved the Lord, his father Saul and the nation of Israel. Jonathan thought of others and had more concern for them than for himself. He not only talked love, he also walked in it—and was more than willing to fight for God's cause.

Does your faith in the Lord spur you to relate to Him in a manner that increases your love and adoration for Him? True love is demonstrated when He is increased and we are decreased.

19. People of faith take it to the enemy.

Jonathan was not willing to sit back and wait for someone else to go after the enemy. He was determined to attack, even if he had to go alone.

Never feel inadequate because "you are only one person." Noah built the ark alone, which was used to save himself and his family. Samson, alone, slew one thousand men with the jawbone of a donkey.

Jonathan made a suggestion to his armor bearer that the two of them go against the Philistine garrison. He could suggest such a thing because he was sold out to the Lord's cause. He wanted victory more than he wanted to live without it, and was no longer willing to allow the prevailing circumstances to continue.

20. People of faith are backed up by the Lord.

When Jonathan told his armor bearer to go with him to fight the Philistines, he agreed. When we take the first step by faith, the Lord will provide help. *"Fear thou not; for I am with thee: be not dismayed; for I am thy God: I will strengthen thee; yea, I will help thee; yea, I will uphold thee with the right hand of my righteousness"* (Isaiah 41:10).

The Lord is with us and He backs us up. We are under His authority, power, care, guidance and protection. He reveals enemy strategies and tactics.

21. People of faith are pleased with God's outcomes.

Jonathan said to his armor bearer, "...the Lord will work for us." He had no doubt as to whether there would be a good outcome. God's way would please him, no matter what happened. If our faith is right, we will accept God's answer, even if the result is different from what we requested.

22. People of faith are not overwhelmed by the odds.

The Philistines had a large army with thousands of chariots and foot soldiers. Human reasoning would conclude it was impossible for Jonathan and his armor bearer to win. True faith-walkers are not overwhelmed by the mountains which tower before them.

Don't worry over the odds. Gideon's army was reduced by God from thirty-two thousand to three hundred men, yet they were victorious. And don't forget about the time the king of Syria sent a host against Elisha (2 Kings 6:17). His servant saw them, and when they surrounded the city, he feared for his life. Then Elisha prayed for

God to open the eyes of the servant, and He did. The servant saw that in the spirit realm, the mountains were full of horses and chariots sent by the Almighty to defeat the foe.

Now it was Jonathan's turn to trust God. He teamed up with his armor bearer to go against the enemy, even though the Philistines appeared to have the advantage.

23. People of faith defy human logic.

Jonathan did something which did not conform to military logic. He suggested that they cross over and let the enemy see them. If the Philistines told them to wait and stand still, they would remain there, but if the Philistines told them to approach, it was a sign the Lord had delivered the enemy into their hands.

By faith we defy human logic. Abraham defeated the confederacy of kings. Jacob became successful in spite of the resistance of Laban. Joseph rose from slavery to statesmanship. Moses saw the Red Sea part and water spew from a rock. Joshua saw the sun stand still by his command. Elijah spoke and the heavens gave no rain or dew for three years.

24. People of faith see the results of their faith.

Jonathan and his armor bearer stepped out in front of the enemy, totally placing their trust in God. When the Philistines saw the two, they ridiculed them and said that they had come out of their holes of hiding.

Some persons may be laughing at us now, but it is not over yet.

The Philistines answered Jonathan and told them to approach. He realized this was the turning point, and told his companion to follow him because the Lord had delivered the enemy into the hands of Israel.

It is clear that he was representing his nation. Jonathan and his armor bearer slew approximately twenty men in an area of about half an acre. Because of their faith, God moved and sent a strong earthquake and tremors throughout the vicinity. The tents of the enemies collapsed, their supplies were scattered, their chariots were damaged. Panic struck the hearts of the entire enemy army and they beat one another down trying to escape. Israel was the victor.

You will never go wrong when you handle the activities of your life in the way the Lord has instructed—even if it seems to baffle logic. I am not advising anyone to act irresponsibly or foolishly, but to move forward when you are sure the direction is from above.

FAITH AND OUTCOMES

Most of us are looking for results in life, so it is helpful to examine the process:

True faith promotes maturity.

As we exercise faith, we experience the miraculous power of God. Our faith actions enable us to endure and overcome every obstacle–and the more this happens the more we grow into maturity.

Our maturity determines our perception.

The point to which we have grown and developed determines our awareness or understanding. When we mature to the place we can see things through the eyes of faith, our perception will be at its peak.

Our perception determines our response.

If we envision by faith, we will see as God sees, act the way God would act, and receive the result that God desires. Our responses should be the result of our faith perceptions.

Our responses determine our strategy.

The way we respond to a problem will determine what we will do in relation to that situation. A fearful response produces a fearful strategy. A reaction of defeat will produce a strategy of defeat. A confused response will produce a confused strategy. But a faith response will produce a plan of faith.

Our strategy determines our outcome.

The approach we take must, by faith, be Spirit led. As believers, our outcome will always be right when we operate under the anointing of God.

A WOMAN WHO BELIEVED

The Old Testament records that as the prophet Elisha journeyed to Shunem there was a woman he was to see. We also learn the faith this Shunammite woman produced was extraordinary (2 Kings. 4:8-11).

25. People of faith become great.

This woman possessed tremendous faith—and this was the essential ingredient to her becoming exceptional in the eyes of Elisha and the Lord. We also learn that greatness is achieved only through obedience to Him, and cannot be measured by earthly standards.

26. People of faith provide for God's appointed servants.

The Shumammite woman arranged for Elisha to visit her house and eat bread. And the prophet accepted. She understood the importance of upholding the man of God. The Bible tells us, *"Thou shalt not muzzle the mouth of the ox that treadeth out the corn"* (1 Timothy 5:18).

Scripture also states that if pastors rule well, they should be worthy of double honor, especially if they labor in the Word and doctrine (1 Timothy 5:17).

27. People of faith recognize those who are real with God.

After Elisha visited her house, the woman perceived he was a holy man who conducted himself in a godly manner and respected her and her husband. She spoke to her spouse concerning setting up a chamber on the wall with a table, stool, and candlestick, with a place to sleep. To do this, they both had confidence in the man of God. They knew Elisha was real with the Lord.

28. People of faith are not forgotten.

Elisha had his servant, Gehazi, bring the Shunammite woman to him. Since she had graciously cared for him, he wanted to find out what he could do for her. She had no special request, but Gehazi told Elisha that her husband was old and she had no children. Elisha told her she would have a son—and the woman conceived and bore a son at the time Elisha said she would.

Our appointed times occur when our preparation is replaced by readiness; when patience will pass the baton to the hand of promise possession; when opposition to fulfillment is defeated; when hope is realized and hindrance is gone; when tears of hardship and pain are overtaken by tears of joy; when the mouths of the skeptics have been silenced and when times of waiting are replaced by times of receiving.

29. People of faith do not fall apart in extreme hardship.

When the woman's child had grown, he went out to his father and the reapers. When he arrived, they boy indicated to his father that something did not feel right in his head. He became sick and they carried him to his mother. He sat on his mother's knees until noon, then he died. Brokenhearted, she went up and laid him on Elisha's bed, shut the door, and left. She prepared to go to Elisha and have him return with her, and told her husband that all would be well. She pressed her way to see the prophet of God.

30. People of faith receive miracles.

Elisha told Gehazi to take his staff and lay it upon the child's face. The mother insisted that Elisha go with her and he did—and the prophet was used by the Lord to raise the boy.

The faith of the woman was her shield of defense until God performed a miracle.

THE FAITH OF PETER IN PRISON

Herod (grandson of Herod the Great who had tried to kill the baby Jesus by murdering the children) became king over Palestine and ruled between A.D. 41-44. He sought popularity with the Jews and pretended to be a Jewish convert—and it was this that caused him to turn against the Church.

Being a shrewd politician, he saw an opportunity to please the Jews by persecuting and seeking to destroy Christian believers. This would keep the Jews quiet and let them support Rome's policies. It would also solidify his power with authorities back in Rome. During this period, in the life of Peter, we learn more about faith-filled people.

31. People of faith will sometimes be vexed.

Herod stretched forth his evil hand to persecute the Church. He killed James, John's brother, and since it pleased the Jews, he proceeded to take Peter. Even though we have faith, we will still at times be persecuted. *"Blesssed are ye, when men shall revile you, and persecute you, and shall say all manner of evil against you falsely, for my sake"* (Matthew 5:11). There are many things in this life that cause aggravation, agitation and grief. As we strive to achieve our goals and dreams, we will experience much resistance in different forms, but despite these things we must persist.

32. People of faith will be apprehended.

The Bible says Herod seized and arrested Peter. In our Christian experience, there will be enemies who will seek to capture and control us. These foes can be in the form of spirit beings, people, habits, attitudes, and more. In one way or another, the enemy will try to stop us because our undertakings (whether ministries, businesses, etc.) will ultimately benefit God's Kingdom.

Because Christ has possessed us, His enemies will pursue us with the intention of causing us to turn from Him. They will seek to steal, kill, and to destroy.

33. People of faith suffer for righteousness sake.

Herod had Peter placed in prison where he was guarded by four quarternions of soldiers—four squads of four soldiers. In such cases one wrist of the prisoner was usually chained to the wrist of a guard. Peter was in prison, yet he had not committed any wrongdoing. He was suffering for the cause of righteousness.

It is clear that Peter understood suffering and how it promotes knowledge of oneself and allows us to discover our true strength or level of maturity. It reveals our measure of faith and our need for the Lord.

We are like olive trees, which were one of the blessings of the Promised Land. Olive trees grow on the mountainside where there is sparse soil—and we develop despite our surrounding conditions. Twenty gallons of oil can be produced by one olive tree—and we also produce much by the power of the Holy Spirit. When harvesting, the branches are shaken and beaten, just as we are shaken and beaten by things we encounter, yet we still produce a bountiful harvest.

The olive was crushed by a stone to release the oil. We must be crushed through our suffering because the will of the flesh must be broken. Peter said, in 1 Peter 5:10, after we have suffered a while, God would make us perfect, establish, strengthen and settle us.

34. People of faith have angelic presence.

The angel of the Lord came to Peter, and a light shined in the prison. As people of faith, we experience angelic presence and assistance. Angels are mentioned in thirty-four books of the Bible for a total of 273 times (108 in the Old and 165 in the New Testament). They are an innumerable, invisible host of spirit beings. Those who did not follow Lucifer are referred to as faithful angels while those who followed him are referred to as fallen angels.

Most Bible scholars believe the angel sent to Peter was the archangel Gabriel. This angel smote Peter on the side, raised him up and told him to get up quickly.

Peter obeyed and the chains fell from his hands while the soldiers remained asleep. The angel told Peter to gather his clothing, put on his shoes, cast his garments about himself, and follow him. Peter followed, but thought he was having a vision.

35. People of faith have doors opened for them.

Peter and the angel passed the first and second ward, then came to the iron gate of the city. The gate opened to them of its own accord and the Lord assured Peter's way out.

By faith, the Lord will open every door necessary, whether spiritual, family, ministry, health, or business related. There is an opening of blessings before us. The gate swung wide and as they passed through the street, the angel departed.

36. People of faith will astonish other believers.

Peter went to the house of Mary, the mother of John, where many were gathered together praying for him. As he knocked on the door, a girl named Rhoda came to see who was there. When she heard Peter's voice, she ran and told the others that he was at the door. They

133

told her she was mad, but when she insisted again, they informed her it was Peter's angel.

Peter continued knocking and when they finally opened the door and saw him, they were astonished. They were praying for Peter, but they did not appear to have expected his release. Too many times in the lives of believers prayer becomes a formality. We often pray without possessing the faith necessary to receive.

37. People of faith glorify God.

When Peter left the prison, he said: "Now I know of a surety, that the Lord hath delivered me out of the hand of Herod, and from all the expectation of the people of the Jews."

When he arrived at Mary's house, he shared with them how the Lord had brought him out of prison. People of faith always give glory and honor to God. They know they could not have accomplished had it not been for Him. As the author Cawdray said: "As the glory of God infinitely transcends man with all his abilities and honors, so it should be in greater esteem than any or all things that can be brought in comparison with it."

Since God has blessed you as only He can, since He has called and saved you, since you are who you are and will become who you are going to be, you should glorify Him.

The greatest triumphs we will ever know are victories of faith. It is not so much what we can do that matters, but what we can trust God to do.

A.B. Simpson wrote: "How often we trust each other, and only doubt our Lord. We take the word of mortals, and yet distrust His Word. But, oh, what light and glory would shine O'er all our days, if we always would remember God means just what He says."

And in the words of D.L. Moody, "Trust in yourself, and you are doomed to disappointment; trust in your friends and they will die and leave you; trust in money, and you may have it taken from you; trust in reputation and some slanderous tongue may blast it; but trust in God, and you are never to be confounded in time or eternity."

Many put their confidence in man because they lack the patience to wait on God.

PETER AND JOHN POSSESSED FAITH

That which took place in Acts 3 is the first recorded miracle of the Church. To attract the attention of the people, the Lord reached down and healed a man whom everyone knew. He blessed the man so much that he went wild with joy and excitement.

It was 3:00 P.M. when Peter and John went up together to the temple in Jerusalem. The early Jewish Christians continued to attend the temple service for a period of time after the Church was formed. The transition and breaking from Judaism was not instantaneous.

38. People of faith are praying people.

Peter and John went to the temple to pray. They likely prayed three specific times daily, not random prayer, nor praying on the run, but at certain hours. Here, they shut the world out and focused solely upon God. Such a prayer life was part of the reason the Lord was able to work through them.

We have faith in God, but the reality of His relationship with us is increased in prayer. Jesus works through those who consistently commune with Him and seek His guidance.

39. People of faith have a heart for hurting people.

A certain man laid at the gate of the temple. He had been lame since his birth. Each day he was carried to the gate called Beautiful to ask for alms of those who entered the temple.

The lame man was over forty years old (Acts 4:22), had never walked and had been continually brought to the temple and placed at the gate to beg. He was probably known by many people, having solicited money for so long. Evidently he had experienced much hardship and grief, yet had learned to live with his condition, though he desired normalcy.

The crippled man is a reminder of our previous condition:

- He was born lame as we were born sinners.
- He could not walk, and as unbelievers we could not walk in a manner pleasing to God.
- He was outside the temple, and before salvation we were outside

of God's temple, the Church.
- He was begging, and while we were in the world we were begging for satisfaction.

When the lame man saw Peter and John he asked them for a gift of charity. Giving to the poor and disabled was considered by the Jews to be an important way to please God. Peter was willing to respond to the man's request.

It is not just enough to see the needs of the world, but it is necessary that we do something. We must help the homeless, imprisoned, poor, needy, and abandoned.

Peter told the beggar to look on them, and at that moment an expectancy was stirred in this lame man. Peter was confident God would use him to heal his condition. He was willing to step out in faith. Perhaps Peter told him to look on them because he was lying there with a pitiful, hopeless expression on his face. In doing so, I believe Peter raised the man's expectation.

The beggar heeded them, expecting to receive something, perhaps silver or gold.

40. People of faith have God-given authority.

Peter said, "Silver and gold have I none; but such as I have give I thee: in the name of Jesus Christ of Nazareth rise up and walk." By faith, Peter was taking authority over the man's sickness.

To call on the name of Jesus means to call upon the authority, power, nature and character of Christ. When Peter said these words, he was proclaiming that the power and authority of Christ Himself would bring healing.

It was a reflection of the fact that the power and presence of Jesus was within him. Peter said, "Such as I have." He had the power and presence of Jesus. It was that which he could give, that which he had to share with sick and hurting individuals.

The Lord was about to use Peter in a mighty way. He took this man by the right hand, lifted him up and immediately his feet and ankles received strength. Notice the human and the divine. Peter helped the man to his feet, then God healed him.

We must do what we can, then the Lord will perform what we

YOU CAN DO IT!

cannot do. The man stood to his feet, then entered into the temple walking, leaping, and praising God. He was completely changed in his whole being, attitude and life. He was no longer shy, reserved, embarrassed, or ashamed.

The man was healed and saved inside and out. He received an unexpected blessing.

- He asked for alms and he received legs.
- He expected the ordinary, but received the extraordinary.
- He expected money, yet received a miracle.
- He expected silver, but received salvation.
- He expected a regular day, yet experienced a special day.
- He expected to receive from earthly givers, but he received from the Divine Giver.
- He expected to be carried home, but he was able to walk home.
- He expected to beg other days, but begged his last day.

The people knew that he was the man who had sat with his hand out at the gate. They were filled with wonder and amazement.

41. People of faith win the unsaved.

The man who had been healed held onto Peter and John. All of the people ran together toward them, wanting to know what had caused such a miracle. This gave Peter the occasion to preach Christ, and he did. The man was won to the Lord, and undoubtedly others were also.

As believers, we know that faith is a higher faculty than reason. It defies human logic. By faith we can achieve things that our minds could never explain. Faith believes God's word for what it cannot see, and is rewarded by seeing what it believes.

George Mueller observed, "The beginning of anxiety is the end of faith, and the beginning of true faith is the end of anxiety." When we believe what God says simply because He said it, fear will be removed.   Someone once said, "Doubt sees the obstacles; faith sees the way. Doubt sees the darkest night; faith sees the day. Doubt dreads to take a step; faith soars on high. Doubt questions, "Who believes?" Faith answers,"I."

FAITH AND A WINNING ATTITUDE

In Philippians 4, Paul said he had learned to be content in whatever state he was in. Looking at the lack in our lives will promote discontentment, and it can cause us to lose focus. It can also foster self-pity, depression, and damaged confidence, which can produce doubt about the future.

Contentment, however, enables us to be aware of what we do not have, without allowing it to offset or defeat us. The presence of faith empowers us to focus upon what we are *going* to have. Faith also reminds us that the loss of a battle is not the loss of the war.

Everything that seems to be a defeat is not. Paul was beaten, stoned, imprisoned and persecuted, but kept a winning attitude because he did not view occurrences as total losses, but as temporary hardships. Do not label yourself a loser simply because you lost a battle. By faith you will achieve the ultimate victory.

42. People of faith are given Kingdom assignments.

The Lord said to Elijah, "Go to Zarephath." He was to discover that he was assigned to be used by the Lord there. Jeremiah was also formed in the womb, born, set apart, and ordained by God for his kingdom assignment as prophet.

Each of us has been ordained by God to perform the functions of our callings. These commissions must be carried out by people of faith. The Lord has invested much in us, and He expects us to fulfill our purposes.

43. People of faith are sustained by the Lord.

The Lord told Elijah that He had commanded a widow woman to sustain him. Elijah was about to be fed in a famine. God is a Sustainer of His people. *"Cast thy burden upon the Lord, and he shall sustain thee: he shall never suffer the righteous to be moved"* (Psalm 55:22).

- He sustained Israel in the wilderness.
- He sustained David on the run from Saul.
- He sustained Job through his suffering.

The woman was about to survive a famine because of her actions of faith.

44. People of faith are blessed for their obedience.

The Bible says that Elijah arose and went to Zarephath. Obedience is the means by which we will stay in the will of God. To obey is to submit to His authority, plans and guidance.

Obedience is the fruit of faith; patience is the blossom *on* the fruit. Dr. J. R. Miller said: "It is a great deal easier to do that which God gives us to do, no matter how hard it is, than to face the responsibilities of not doing it."

45. People of faith will always keep God first.

When Elijah came to the gate of the city, he saw a widow woman gathering sticks. Though death seemed to be on her doorstep, she still did what she could. Elijah called to her and said, "Fetch me, I pray thee, a little water in a vessel, that I may drink." As she was going to fetch it, Elijah called to her and said, "Bring me, I pray thee, a morsel of bread in thine hand."

The woman responded she only had a handful of meal in a barrel and a little oil in a cruse. She was going to prepare the last meal for herself and her son, eat, and they were going to die. Elijah told her not to fear, but to go and make him a little cake first.

This was a test of circumstances. The woman was now face to face with starvation. As far as she was concerned only a handful of meal was between her and the grave. Elijah shows his faith in God's promise that he would be sustained, by persisting in having the first portion. He told the woman not to be fearful.

Did not Jesus ask a drink of the woman of Samaria, knowing that He had something better to give. The Lord sometimes asks us for our last so we can establish a continual flow. He must be first. Matthew 6:33 informs us that if we give the Lord priority, our needs and desires will be provided.

The woman went and did as Elijah requested. He gave her the Lord's promise that the meal in the barrel would not end nor the cruse of oil fail until the famine ceased. She believed the word and prepared the last morsel of food for Elijah. Putting God first manifests our love

139

for Him, our faith in Him, our submission to Him and our desire to see His kingdom advanced.

46. People of faith see their little become much.

The woman had a very small amount of meal. At God's bidding, she gave all that she had, and cast herself entirely upon the promise of God. She did not have any precedent for such an act, yet she had faith in the Lord. Blessed are they who have not seen and yet have believed.

Elijah told her the Lord had said the meal and oil would not run out until He sent rain. According to the word of Elijah, she and her son ate many days. Neither the meal or the oil failed. She saw her little become much—and God will do the same for us.

CHAPTER 5

ABUNDANCE
IS IN YOUR GRASP

Most believers speak of the abundant life, but not enough seem to achieve it. If Jesus came so we could receive such a blessing, why are there so many who are not enjoying this privilege?

The walk of the Christian is not supposed to be one of lack, slack, and living in the back! Whatever our previous state of existence, it should improve when we come to Christ. He intends for each of His children to come to the comforting realization of what He has provided for them. Yet many never experience this great truth. They simply reason, everybody is not going to be rich"—viewing abundance only in terms of money, and lack a consideration of spiritual abundance. Yet what the Lord promised is for all, not *some*.

It is important for us to examine the nature of the abundant life. It is superior in quality and beyond measure. It excels all other lifestyles and gives us the advantage. Even more, it guarantees total prosperity and can only be given by the Lord.

GOD'S GUARANTEE

This abundance is experienced in both the spiritual and the natural realms. Spiritually, it is provided for those who are born again. As a result, we are in a more favorable position than those outside of Christ. We are enjoying a walk with the Lord we otherwise cannot experience naturally—a heavenly power which gives us advantage and a spiritual life that guarantees our prosperity.

We have abundance because the blessings of our spiritual lives flow into our natural lives. Contrary to the opinion of some, believers should prosper in their physical walk.

The Lord has the leading role in our prosperity. Jesus makes this clear when He states, *"I am come that they might have life, and that they might have it more abundantly"*(John 10:10)

When He says, "I am come," it indicates Jesus is the personal deliverer of all that is necessary for our abundance. He alone has the power to deliver it, knowledge of how to accomplish it and only He can bestow this upon every believer.

Even more, in order to deliver this blessing, Jesus first had to possess it—and only He has such authority. Christ is the promoter of this favor, establishing the means by which it comes to us. He promoted it through the sacrifice of His life, through the recording of His word, through the power of His Spirit for us to achieve and through the rights and privileges of believers.

Jesus is the producer of abundance—the One who gave birth and brought it into existence. Without Him there could be no production of it in our lives. He instructs us in what to do, and when we follow His guidance, His bountiful blessings descend.

Since He brings this favor, no one can abort its presence.

Let's look at the Lord's attitude toward abundance:

First: He desires this for His people.

"Beloved, I wish above all things that thou mayest prosper and be in health, even as thy soul prospereth" (3 John 2). These are the words John prayed for Gaius, a church leader—that he would be prosperous and fulfilled all of his days.

God has a divine desire that we achieve abundance. *"The Lord is my shepherd; I shall not want"* (Psalm 23:1). He does not plan for us to live a life of lack. *"He maketh me to lie down in green pastures: he leadeth me beside the still waters"* (v.2). We are told: *"Delight thyself also in the Lord; and he shall give thee the desires of thine heart"* (Psalm 37:4).

Second: He also designed this for His people.

The life of a believer is carried on in a plan created by God. In Psalm 1, the psalmist gives several keys to success.

One: He gives us the abundance posture. It is a walk that is not in the counsel of the ungodly. It is directed by the Holy Spirit.

Two: It is a stand that is not in the way of sinners. We do not fraternize or spend time inappropriately with unbelievers. We do not isolate ourselves, rather we witness to them and seek to lead them to Christ

Three: It is a place that is not in the seat of the scornful or those who mock the things of God. The imagery of this scripture presents an ideal righteous person, one who is in the world, yet unaffected by its enticements. The parallelism in the verse reveals an increasingly deeper involvement with wickedness, walking beside, to standing with, to sitting beside. Similarly, the terms for the wicked are progressive, ungodly, sinners, and scornful.

Third: He gives us abundant pleasure.

Those who will receive God's abundance will delight in His law. We receive pleasure and satisfaction from our study of the Word and are made joyful in its reading. Instead of finding gratification in entanglements with the wicked, we find our deep enjoyment in the things of God, particularly His Word. We meditate and engage in deep and serious reflection on what He has written. In the process, we empty our minds of distracting thoughts and fix our attention on Him. Certainly, we attend to other responsibilities, but our priority is the Lord.

Fourth: He gives us abundant placement.

The Lord says we are like a tree planted by the rivers of water. We have a never-ending supply of nourishment and refreshment—and we bring forth fruit. Planting signifies our stability. The image is that of a desert date palm tree which has been firmly planted in a well watered oasis. In the middle of a dry and sinful world, we bring forth what is good. We are valuable and productive to God and His people.

Fifth: He gives us abundant prosperity.

Our leaves shall not wither, meaning our lives are not governed by cyclical changes. I love the quote of D. L. Moody when he said, "All of the Lord's trees are evergreen."

Whatever we do shall prosper because we are planted in Christ. His leadership directs us only to avenues of blessing.

Our abundance is also decreed by God. He foreordained it before we were born, according to the counsel of His own will. This command is eternal and wise since it is a product of His infinite wisdom and free from external input or influence.

Since the law of abundance was established in eternity past, no one advised or convinced Him to grant it. There was a set time for the coming of our abundance to begin and continue. Christ paved the way with the sacrifice of His life, and all who come to Him arrive at their perfect time for His blessing.

Since it has been decreed, it must be fulfilled without fail during our lifetime. There is no occurrence which can suspend any of the relationships or conditions under which this covenant is to be completed. Though we have the ability to choose, in the omniscience of God it was all a part of His eternal declaration. In view of this, we can only conclude that God foreordained our abundance. By His wisdom, He assured it would happen. By His power it is brought to pass in our lives. By His authority it is unconditional and against all resistance.

HE WILL BRING IT TO PASS

It is imperative for every believer to have the right attitude concerning abundance. Since God offers this, we need to be open to accept what has already been provided. As the Almighty spoke through the words of the prophet Isaiah, *"...I have spoken it, I will also bring it to pass; I have purposed it, I will also do it"* (Isaiah 46:11).

This verse speaks both of the power of God's spoken words and His ability to perform what He has declared. When He said He came to bring us abundant life, He spoke it. And the fulfillment of the spoken word is no more reliable than the character of the one speaking.

Remember, The Lord declared in the above verse, "I will bring it to pass." He will personally see to it that what He has spoken will happen. When He speaks, the forces of His creation must respond and everything is aligned for it to occur. No resistance can alter it, and we

YOU CAN DO IT!

can know with assurance it will be.

However, we receive God's promises only if we meet His conditions (Deuteronomy 28). His blessings are not automatically poured out upon us. God is not a heavenly robot that impulsively responds on the spur of the moment without thought or purpose. His favor is not granted randomly in a chaotic manner.

The Father requires our obedience to Him. *"If my people, which are called by my name, shall humble themselves, and pray, and seek my face, and turn from their wicked ways; then will I hear from heaven, and will forgive their sin, and will heal their land"* (2 Chronicles 7:14). He also tells us, *"If thou wilt diligently hearken to the voice of the Lord thy God, and wilt do that which is right in his sight, and wilt give ear to his commandments, and keep all his statutes, I will put none of these diseases upon thee"* (Exodus 15:26).

Here is one more example of the conditions He demands: *"If ye hearken to these judgments, and keep, and do them, that the Lord thy God shall keep unto thee the covenant and the mercy which he sware unto thy fathers: and he will love thee, and bless, thee, and multiply thee: he will also bless the fruit of thy womb, and the fruit of thy land, thy corn, and thy wine, and thine oil..."* (Deuteronomy 7:12-13).

In each of these situations, the blessings were to be received if the required conditions were met.

THE "IF" FACTOR

In Deuteronomy 28 the Lord itemized blessings that would come to Israel if obedience was evident. He said, *"And it shall come to pass, if thou shalt hearken diligently unto the voice of the Lord thy God, to observe and to do all his commandments which I command thee this day, that the Lord thy God will set thee on high above all nations."*

When the "if" question is settled, the Lord would bless them as follows:

- Blessings would come on them and overtake them.
- They would be blessed in the city and in the field.
- They would be fruitful in their bodies, in their ground, in their

145

cattle and in the flocks of their sheep.
- They would be blessed in their basket and in their store.
- They would be blessed coming in and going out.
- Their enemies would be smitten before their faces.
- He would command the blessing upon their storehouses, and in all they set their hands to do.
- He would establish them as a holy people unto Himself.
- He would make them plenteous in goods.
- He would open to them His good treasure.
- He would make them the head and not the tail, above and not beneath.
- He would make them the lenders, not the borrowers.

Personally, I have found that my walk of obedience has provided me with many blessings that I was unable to previously enjoy. The Lord has favored us in many ways, so the least we can do is be obedient to Him.

WHAT COMES FIRST?

Our attitude should also be that we will use the abundance to benefit God's Kingdom—not for personal gain alone. Matthew 6:33 says, *"But seek ye first the kingdom of God, and his righteousness; and all these things shall be added unto you."*

What does it mean to seek the Kingdom? It means to worship God, to be about His business, putting forth serious effort in our service to Him, to inquire and discover more about Him and to discover ways to benefit His kingdom.

Genuine concern for the work of the Lord is not easily found today. So many Christians seem to be wrapped up in providing for themselves to the neglect of God's house. When king Jehoash was repairing the temple, funds were needed (2 Kings 12:4-8,10-14) and the people brought monies for the repairs to be made. They presented so much the priests had to tell them not to bring any more. The funds were given to the workers for the performance of the work.

Our abundance and prosperity must be used to assure that all of the needs of the Church are met. Ministries have mortgages, salaried employees, gas and electric, equipment purchases, insurance, building repairs, and more. Plus the maintenance involved.

The Church could have an expanded work in the world if Christians would properly give of their resources as they are financially blessed. Surely, when we seek the Lord first, we will prosper.

AN ETERNAL AGREEMENT

Our approach should be that we will remember we are covenant people. A covenant is an agreement between two persons or two groups that involves promises on the part of each to the other. The New Covenant is the agreement God has made with mankind, based on the death and resurrection of Jesus Christ. Jesus' sacrificial death served as the oath, or pledge, that God made to us to seal this bond.

The New Testament, which itself means "new covenant," interprets the work of Jesus Christ as bringing this into being. In His death, Jesus ushered in the new covenant and now we are justified by God's grace and mercy.

When we give our lives to Christ and walk in obedience to Him, we become positioned for the fulfillment of God's promises. When we do our part, He does His—in addition to what He has already provided. Instead of dwelling on every difficulty that arises, perhaps we should focus upon our covenant benefits including, but not limited to, the following:

- Abundant life (John.10:10).
- Answers to prayer (1 John. 5:14).
- Power for service (John 14:12).
- Companionship (John.15:15).
- Everlasting life (John. 3:16).
- Deliverance (2 Timothy 4:18).
- God's protecting care (1 Peter 5:6-7).
- Liberty (Romans 8:2).
- Fellowship with Jesus (Matthew18:19).
- Rewards (Matthew 10:42).
- Inheritance (1 Peter 1:3-4).

- Hope (Hebrews 6:18-19).

THE RESISTORS

"The thief cometh not, but for to steal, and to kill, and to destroy..." (John 10:10). This scripture is clear evidence there will be planned resistance to our abundance. Notice that the verse does not say *"a* thief," but *"the* thief." Satan himself is being spoken of here. He comes to any situation where he can inflict harm and has a strategy to achieve his evil.

Some try to deny his existence, but the Bible declares he is real. The devil is mentioned in at least seven Old Testament books (Genesis, 1 Chronicles, Job (12 times), Psalms, Isaiah, Ezekiel and Zechariah). His origin and fall are documented in Ezekiel 28:11-19 and in Isaiah 14:12-15.

At the time of his fall, he and all of the angels who sided with him against the Lord, were cast out of heaven. Satan has a personality, and he is a real being, possessing intelligence a will and emotions.

His organizational skills are significant. He led the first rebellion against God. Also, the devil will orchestrate and lead the last rebellion against the Almighty. He comes to steal more than natural possessions from us. It is his desire to strip us of our love, joy, peace, longsuffering, gentleness, goodness, faith, meekness, and temperance. Plus, it is the devil's plan to steal our abundance and happiness.

He comes to kill, both spiritually and naturally—to destroy our lives, ministries, families, careers, health, businesses, and more.

The enemy came against Job's abundance. But remember, God *allowed* Satan to test Job's faithfulness. Here was a man who was blameless, upright, a man of wealth and integrity who possessed an abundance of faith.

WHY ATTACKS COME

Job owned 7,000 sheep, 3,000 camels, 500 yoke of oxen, 500 donkeys, many servants, houses and land. In fact, he was the richest man in his entire area. He also possessed a large family—a wife, seven sons, and three daughters.

Enemy attacks must not be taken to mean a person has committed sin. They could be a manifestation of our weaknesses (Job was fearful about the lifestyle of his sons). Also, they can be a reflection of God's confidence in our maturity. Attacks can only come to us if He permits them.

In the length of just one day Job experienced four terrible tragedies. (1) The Sabeans stole all of his oxen, donkeys, and killed his farmhands. (2) Fire fell from heaven and burned his sheep and shepherds. (3) The Chaldeans carried off his camels and killed his servants. And (4) a mighty wind blew down the house where his sons and daughters were, killing all of them.

These combined events took place with God's permission.

Job's friends had opinions concerning his situation. Eliphaz, Bildad and Zophar assumed his sin was the cause of Job's calamities. Elihu, a younger man, urged Job to humble himself and submit to God's will, and rebuked Job for unjustly accusing the Lord.

Job developed boils from his head to his toes, and his wife suggested he curse God and die. He told her that she spoke like a foolish woman.

Through all of these trials, and his anguish with the Lord, Job still held on to his trust in the Almighty:

- He was able to endure material loss (camels, sheep, oxen, donkeys and a house).
- He was able to endure human loss (his shepherds, servants, and herdsmen).
- He was able to endure family loss (seven sons, three daughters).
- He was able to endure his wife's betrayal and the negativity of his friends.

There are times it seems almost impossible to continue because nothing is happening to advance our lives. Progress is lost and we may have to start over. Our friends have drawn their own conclusions and family members have counted us out. We say to ourselves, "If one more thing happens, it's over!"

Despite all this, I am letting you know, "You *can* do it!"

As long as there is breath in your body, never consider yourself finished or defeated. The answer to your dilemma is not always found in those who are around you. The Lord has so positioned you in Him that you are empowered to achieve, even if all seems hopeless.

When we walk in spiritual and natural abundance, it infuses us with durability, determination, and a complete disregard for negative influences.

The abundant life is productive and will yield only what is good.

A DOUBLE BLESSING

The Lord showed Job he could not understand His divine government. God had a deep interest in the affairs of this man, and Job had to realize his own smallness and God's unlimited greatness.

When the storm passed, the Lord blessed the latter days of Job more than his beginning. He was healed and he received "double" for his losses. He received 14,000 sheep, 6,000 camels, 1000 yoke of oxen, 1,000 she asses. He was also blessed with seven sons and three more daughters. Job lived one hundred and forty more years and saw his sons, his grandsons, even four generations.

Job achieved amazing abundance in both his spiritual and natural life, despite all the enemy threw against him.

THE DECEIVER

The various names of the Evil One in scripture reflect his nature:

1. Devil (1 John 3:8).
2. Deceiver (Revelation 20:10).
3. Belial (2 Corinthians 6:15).
4. Wicked one (Matthew13:38).
5. Tempter (1 Thessalonians 3:5).
6. Accuser of the brethren (Revelation 12:10).
7. Liar (John 8:44).
8. Murderer (John 8:44).
9. Enemy (Matthew 13:39).
10. Roaring lion (1 Peter 5:8).

His activities are anti-Christ:
1. He instigates false doctrine (1 Timothy 4:1-3).
2. He perverts God's Word (Genesis 3:1-4).
3. He blinds people to the truth (2 Corinthians 4:4).
4. He resists the prayers of believers (Daniel10:12).
5 He afflicts (Job 2:7).
6. He lays snares (2 Timothy 2:26).
7. He tempts (Matthew 4:1).
8. He deceives (Revelation 20:10).

As born again believers, we must remember that Satan and his entire host have limitations. The Bible reveals the powerful creature he is, but in spite of all his influence and ability, the devil is still a created being—not the Creator. This means his power and knowledge are definitely limited.

He is not omnipotent. Satan's true strength is like that of a flea against a rhinoceros when compared to God's strength—like a mosquito against an elephant.

He is not omnipresent and cannot be everywhere at the same time. He has to use millions of fallen angels to achieve his devious goals.

He is not omniscient. He has accumulated a large amount of knowledge because he has been around for at least six thousand years, yet he does not know the future or the secrets of the past.

If Satan has read the Word, he already knows he will lose. He could be aware of biblical prophecies, but according to Ezekiel 28:17, sin has corrupted Satan's wisdom to the extent he still thinks he will defeat God. However, we have victory over Satan. *"These things I have spoken unto you, that in me you might have peace. In the world ye shall have tribulation: but be of good cheer; I have overcome the world"* (John 16:33). And we are told, *"Ye are of God, little children, and have overcome them: because greater is he that is in you, than he that is in the world"* (1 John 4:4).

Our victory over the enemy is assured. Satan and his demonic powers may resist our increasing abundance, but they can never stop it.

151

WHAT KIND OF PROSPERITY?

Our abundance is also resisted by improper traditional views which are established as a result of the handing down of information, beliefs, customs, inherited practices or opinions. Also, they are established by cultural continuity in attitudes and institutions.

Some time-honored traditional views are definitely good. For example, the one of marriage between a man and a woman is not only proper, it is biblical. The long-standing opinion of the need for family unity is also healthy.

Others, however, need to be evaluated. One traditional opinion in the church that needs to be adjusted concerns walking in prosperity and abundance. As I have mentioned, some still believe Christians should not enjoy material abundance; that financial wealth will corrupt believers and cause them to be lost.

Let's establish the fact that before any other type of prosperity, there must be *spiritual* prosperity. The emphasis should always be placed upon the development of a quality spiritual relationship with the Lord. This must always take preference over money and material possessions.

Also, our spiritual position should not be measured by wealth or belongings. The apostle Paul lived in spiritual abundance, though much of the time he experienced lack in material possessions, and even sought financial assistance from some of the churches he founded.

However, I do believe blessings will come to our natural lives when we give preeminence to the Lord. As a matter of fact, the persons He prospers are positioned to be major contributors to the expansion of the work of the Lord's Kingdom.

THE PROMISE OF THE WORD

Our abundance is resisted by non-biblical lifestyles. If the abundant life is to be achieved, it must be attained God's way. To disregard the Word is to preclude oneself from experiencing the life of plenty God envisions. The Bible is God's Word and we must be sure to adhere to its commands. The world's best seller was written as the

YOU CAN DO IT!

Spirit of the Lord moved upon the writers. It has amazing unity, is indestructible, is historically, scientifically and prophetically accurate and has universal influence. Most important, the Word has life changing power.

The Word of God is inerrant and our obedience to it assures us of the abundant life. Nothing can be seen as love to God which is not shaped through submission.

Here's what obedience does. It::

- Maintains our fellowship with the Lord and brings His favor.
- Promotes purpose fulfillment and enables us to be used by the Lord.
- Places and keeps us in harmony with God's will and makes us effective in all we do.
- Promotes total prosperity and assures us of a life of walking in blessing.

WRONG THINKING

Our abundance is resisted by improper mindsets.

Wrong thinking invites doubt, discouragement and a desire to fail. It tells us we cannot do what faith says we can, and makes situations appear to be too difficult. It tries to convince us that we will never bounce back from setbacks and that trying situations will never change. Also, wrong thinking will lead us to believe that everyone else is doing better than we are, and God is not going to come through for us—that we are stuck at our current place of hardship, and that is where we will stay.

Finally, it tries to make us believe we are too far down to rise up and walk in abundance, but we can do it. Paul said in Philippians 4:13, *"I can do all things through Christ which strengtheneth me."*

When we make such a declaration and face our circumstances, Jesus will step in and give us the strength to press on to victory.

CONNECTED TO THE PROPHET

God informed Elijah that Elisha was to be his successor. As a sign,

Elijah went to this young man and threw his mantle on him.

In actuality, for Elisha this was a word from the Lord. When this event occurred, he requested to go home and prepare a farewell feast for his family. After he did so, he arose and went to the great prophet and became his personal servant.

Elisha was striving for spiritual abundance. The fact he had twelve yoke of oxen indicates he was not poor in the natural.

You too have received a word from the Lord. Jesus has already declared He came so you could have a more abundant life. To achieve it, however, we must step out on His word as Elisha did.

He left his family and his home to obtain what the Lord ordained. Elisha did not receive his increase the moment it was spoken to him. He had to trust God's Word and take a giant leap forward.

Elijah told Elisha he was his successor, but Elisha had to *believe* it. To receive what the Lord had for him, it was necessary to follow God's directives.

Elisha connected with the one who could help him obtain the increase which was promised.

After the two left Gilgal, on three different occasions—Bethel, Jericho and Jordan—Elijah tried to get Elisha to wait for him until he returned from those locations. But each time, Elisha told the prophet, "I will not leave you."

Finally Elijah asked Elisha what he could do for him before he was taken up to heaven. Elisha requested, "I want a double portion of your spirit."

The prophet told Elisha that if he saw him when he was taken up, his request would be granted. I believe Elisha was so determined to receive what the Lord had promised him that he refused to sleep—watching and waiting every waking moment.

A chariot of fire appeared and parted them, and Elijah went up by a whirlwind into heaven. Elisha witnessed this and took up the mantle of Elijah. His request was granted, and when he went back to the Jordan, he smote the waters and they parted.

We must also give priority to receiving our abundance and persist as Elisha did. He not only received a double portion of Elijah's spirit, but if you read the scriptures, you'll find he performed twice as many miracles as Elijah.

Remember, this concerning abundance. It has been provided for you, yet it must be decided by you to possess and keep. For by your sowing you will reap.

ACHIEVING THE ABUNDANT LIFE

Here are three reasons we receive the life God has graciously promised:

1. We achieve abundance because we do things God's way.

We are free moral agents, which means we have the God-given ability to make choices. This being true, we can decide to do things the Father's way, or map our own course.

By opening His book and listening to His voice we will be guided to the path which leads to His blessings.

2. We achieve abundance because we follow the directives of the Holy Spirit.

As Spirit-filled believers, we are empowered to resist everything that will come to harm us or stop our abundance. Acts 1:8 promises we will have power after the Holy Ghost comes upon us. He provides a wall of protection around our lives which limits Satan's attacks against us.

He teaches, strengthens, guides, enables us to love, prays for us, reveals Biblical truth, gives liberty, conforms us to the image of Christ, and so much more.

3. We achieve abundance because we have the favor of God.

The outpouring of the Father's favor supplies us in a manner we do not deserve. It makes it possible for us to achieve what we could not achieve normally, and to become what we could never have become on our own.

- Peter was favored and rose from fisherman to a Chief Apostle who carried the gospel to the Gentiles.
- Paul was favored and was used by God to evangelize the world during his time.

155

- Abraham was favored and was made the father of a nation.
- Jacob was favored and became the father of the heads of the tribes of Israel.
- Joseph was favored and rose to second in command in Egypt.
- Solomon was favored and was blessed with wisdom beyond all other men.

The Lord's blessing gives us the advantage over our enemies. It makes the impossible become possible through the power of the Holy Spirit. It turns losers into winners and the defeated into the victorious. Today, you can start living and enjoying the abundant life.

CHAPTER 6

YOUR BEST DAYS
ARE JUST AHEAD

I f you were asked to make a list of the major events in your life, what would it include?

As we review our past we find certain happenings have been wonderful, some horrible and others just plain ridiculous. There are facts we must accept:

- There have been successes and failures.
- Many have experienced divorces and separations.
- Others have suffered major illnesses.
- Some have lost close friends and relatives to death.
- Others have plummeted to life's lowest points.
- There have been times we were not treated fairly.

But what about our attitude concerning the present? Here are some actions we all need to take:

- We need to acknowledge we are where we are because He has blessed us.
- We need to, with God's help, overcome the hurts and abuses of the past.
- We need to learn to be content where we are until God brings change.
- We need to use our current time to prepare for our future.
- We need to keep our focus on the fulfillment of our destiny.

- We need to work for the Lord while we can.
- We need to live with great expectation of our better days.

Through all of our journey, we must conclude that God has been good to us. Every past and present experience has been a part of our preparation to become who we are and who we will become tomorrow.

The most exciting news of all is that your best days are still ahead. This is not just wishful thinking, but a reality based on the promises of God's Word. On these pages we've talked about the purpose for which you were created and your Kingdom assignment, however, what the Lord is preparing for your future far outweighs anything we can ask or think.

DON'T OVERLOOK TODAY!

Instead of twiddling our thumbs while we are waiting, there are some specific activities in which God expects us to be engaged.

1. Pray in the present.

Communion with the Lord will promote a quality relationship with Him. It conditions our hearts and minds for where the Lord is taking us and for what He is going to do on our behalf. Prayer anchors us in Christ and helps us resist the enemy. Through prayer we receive and maintain a godly appetite and are spiritually edified.

This is why the Word tells us to *"Pray without ceasing"* (1 Thessalonians 5:17).

2. Seek peace in the present.

In this fast paced, terror infested world, there must be an inner calm to stabilize us. This is essential to keep us from operating in confusion. As we move toward our best days, God's perfect rest will bring tranquility when it is needed.

If we lose our peace, we will lose our joy of the Lord which is our strength and fortress. In the words of an old axiom, "Peace will rule our days when Christ rules our minds." It's true. *"Thou wilt keep him in perfect peace, whose mind is stayed on thee: because he trusteth in thee"* (Isaiah 26:3).

3. Be persistent in the present.

There must be a resolve residing within us to forge ahead despite the opposition. I'm speaking of a determination to stay in the battle and to endure "hardness" as a good soldier of Christ.

With the apostle Paul, we need to declare, *"I press toward the mark for the prize of the high calling of God in Christ Jesus"* (Philippians 3:14).

4. Be patient in the present.

If you truly believe the best is yet to come, you can keep your composure during the period of waiting. The Word tells us, *"But if we hope for that we see not, then do we with patience wait for it"* (Romans 8:25).

Remember, only through faith and patience can we inherit the precious promises (Hebrews 6:12).

5. Receive power in the present.

When Jesus told the disciples and early believers to wait in Jerusalem for the promise of the Father, He was speaking of the Holy Spirit—which descended on those in the Upper Room with awesome power. This was not exclusively for the early church; it is for us today!

The Holy Spirit is available to help you successfully engage in spiritual warfare and lead you into all truth.

WHAT'S NEXT?

The reason we know our finest days are coming is because the Lord has gone before us and determined our path. As the psalmist declared, *"Thou wilt shew me the path of life"* (Psalm 16:11).

The Father has defined our goals and if we will seek Him, He will make it clear what we are to achieve. Plus, He has provided the resources we need to enter into our days of triumph.

We can also rest assured that He has defeated our enemies. Jesus declared, *"...All power is given unto me in heaven and in earth"*

(Matthew 28:18). This includes power over Satan and his demons. Our outcome has been determined since we know:

- The Lord is our Shepherd (Psalm 23:1).
- He maketh us to lie down in green pastures (v.2).
- He will abundantly satisfy us with the "fatness" of His house (Psalm 36:8).
- His eyes are upon us and His ears are open to our cries (Psalm 34:15).
- He preserves the faithful and rewards the proud doer (Psalm 31:23).
- He is our light and salvation (Psalm 27:5).

THE LORD'S SURPRISING PLANS

In the third year of his reign, King Ahasuerus hosted a great feast. He invited the princes, servants and nobles of the provinces, using this occasion to display the riches of his kingdom.

The king ordered his chamberlains to bring Queen Vashti, who was entertaining the women at a separate banquet. He wanted her to make a grand entrance so he could show off her beauty—just as he had exhibited his wealth. In essence, he was asking her to degrade herself to satisfy his drunken desire.

Vashti declined, and her refusal angered her husband. The invited men told Ahasuerus that Vashti's unwillingness to obey would set a bad example for other women. They suggested she be removed as Queen by a royal decree. The king, humiliated, rashly signed the edict into law and Vashti was ousted.

When the king's anger subsided, he may have had second thoughts over what he had done to Vashti, but the decree had already been signed. To fill the royal void, his servants suggested that all of the beautiful young virgins of the country be sought out, then one of them would be selected to become the next queen.

This plan was carried out and all of the selected females were gathered together, taken to Shushan, and placed in the care of Hegai, the king's chamberlain. As we will see, this period of history was not kind to Jewish people, and they longed for better days.

The Lord elevates us.

The subjects of the kingdom didn't yet know it, but Vashti had to be removed because someone of God's choosing was destined for the throne.

The Lord caused the beauty contest to take place and preordained that a Jewish girl by the name of Esther would be selected as the winner. God also planned that she find favor with the king when she went into his presence during the contest.

God is also working on our behalf. At this very moment He is arranging for our success in our homes, workplaces, communities and in our ministries. He is getting approvals, breakthroughs, increases, promotions, and all things for our benefit.

The Lord orders our steps.

Esther had a cousin named Mordecai. His destiny was planned by the Lord so he would be exactly where he was when the people of Israel were taken into captivity. Their steps were ordered so they would be in Shushan at the time of Vashti's expulsion. The Lord knew He would need both Mordecai and Esther in that place at the appointed hour, and allowed them to reside there during this period.

God's road for us is always the best path, even if it does not seem that way. It is good to know the difference between God's ordering and self-ordering.

The Lord opens doors for us.

When Esther was brought into the king's house to Hegai, keeper of the women, she impressed him. God gave Esther favor with this man and he treated her kindly. He quickly gave her what was needed for her purification—ointments, spices and cosmetics. He also offered her seven maidens from the king's house to assist her, and arranged for Esther to have the preferred place in the house of the women.

The opening of such doors of privilege can only be provided by the Lord. I regularly declare by faith that doors are opening for me and I daily *expect* them to. Portals of opportunity lie in my future and through spiritual eyes I see the gates swing open wide.

The Lord prepares people to help us.

God made sure Mordecai was present to help Esther. He mentored, advised, prayed and interceded for her. Each day he walked before the court of the women's house to see how she was progressing in the contest. However, Mordedai wisely advised her not to reveal that she was Jewish because their people were not politically correct at the time.

We all need one another, and the Lord will raise up people to help us—and will call us to assist others:

- Lot had Abraham.
- Joseph had the butler.
- Joshua had Moses.
- David had Jonathan.
- Nehemiah had Artaxerxes.

Certain people in our lives have been placed there by God, and when He is ready to use them on our behalf, He will direct them to provide the assistance we need. If we stay humble, we will recognize the Lord's hand in our circumstances and work harmoniously with others.

GET READY FOR A TRANSFORMATION

It is vital that we prepare for change.

The purification program which groomed the young ladies lasted twelve months. After this, each contestant awaited her turn to go before the king.

We, too, must go through a period of preparation for our best days. Life should be considered a *training* time for our *reigning* time!

Every day you need to make positive predictions and declarations of what lies ahead. Don't be afraid to speak out and tell others of your hopes and expectations. The faith that causes you to visualize, will allow you to both prophesy and prepare for your coming achievement. If you believe in your dream, you will make ready for its reality.

Time to be Presented

Esther participated in every step of the process—and so must we. While we are waiting on the Lord, we are to consistently and continually be involved in the work of His Kingdom. Our participation must be fervent in the work, the warfare and in the worship of the Lord. When I see, by faith, what God is about to do with my life, it automatically prompts excitement in me to take part and do more.

It is also important to realize we will be *presented* before the Lord when we reach the culmination of our best days.

When the moment arrived for a young lady to go before the king, she could request anything for her adornment so she could look her finest. Then she was ready to spend an evening with the king. But if she failed to please him, she would never be in his presence again.

Esther, however, did not ask for additional adornments and went into the royal chamber with her natural beauty. The Bible tells us she obtained the favor of the king and all who looked upon her. *"And the king loved Esther above all the women, and she obtained grace and favour in his sight more than all the virgins; so that he set the royal crown upon her head, and made her queen instead of Vashti"* (Esther 2:17).

For some of us, our time is now; for others it is soon to come. Through every test you have become more prepared. At the appointed moment, because of your obedience, you will be presented before the Lord.

Do What's Right

God positions us today for the battles of tomorrow.

Mordecai set himself strategically at the palace gate and on one occasion he overheard a plot to assassinate the king. Two of the king's chamberlains were angry and sought to kill the leader, but Mordecai reported it to Esther, who in turn told King Ahasuerus.

When an investigation took place, both men were apprehended, given a trial, and hanged. The incident was routinely recorded in the official chronicles of the palace. At that time, Mordecai was not rewarded, yet his kind deed of warning on behalf of the king would prove to be extremely beneficial later.

You cannot afford to become discouraged and angry just because it seems you are not being properly honored. Don't become disheartened when you significantly help those who are doing better than yourself and they do nothing to show their appreciation. Continue to do what is right and know that our God is a just rewarder of His people. As we will see, Mordecai's deed was a seed which ultimately produced a bountiful harvest for him and his people.

EXPECT OPPOSITION

There is another player in the story—a man named Haman. He is indicative of the negatives that work against us.

Some time after the event when Mordecai reported the planned assignation of Ahasuerus, the king promoted Haman. He was an Agagite, a descendant of the kings of the Amalekites. The Lord had declared ongoing war against Amalek (Exodus 17:8-16).

The king proclaimed Haman's authority to be above the princes, and all the king's servants bowed and reverenced him—as was commanded. Mordecai, however, did neither.

Haman was an egotistical, evil individual who devised a scheme to annihilate all the Jews in the kingdom. He was cruel and an enemy of God and His people.

On the other end of the spectrum was Mordecai, a man of conviction who was persuaded to only serve the God of Israel. In him we can see the traits of Christ:

- He adopted Esther, which shows mercy (Esther. 2:7). We were predestined to be adopted by Jesus Christ (Ephesians 1:5).
- Mordecai was faithful to the king. Jesus was faithful to the Father (Luke. 2:49).
- He was consistent. Jesus steadfastly set His face toward Jerusalem for the purpose of sacrificing Himself (Luke 9:51).

- Mordecai was despised (Esther 3:5). Jesus was despised (Isaiah 53:3).
- He was tested (Esther. 4:1). Jesus was tested (Matthew 4:1-11).
- He received a place of honor. Jesus also received a place of honor upon His resurrection.

THE "DEATH DECREE"

We will all encounter Hamans in our lives. They are individuals who do all they can to stop us, and nothing to assist us. They refuse to celebrate our victories or successes and crave the power and honor which is due to others. Such people are envious of anyone who exceeds them and will organize strategies to overthrow them. They do not care if they destroy individuals or families.

When "Hamans" show up, remember they can only come by God's permission and are present because the Lord allows them to be. He will use them to build us up, not to harm us. They are indications we are effective in God's work.

The king's servants asked Mordecai why he was disobeying the king's law—then informed Haman that Mordecai would not bow and that he was an Israelite. Haman was consumed with anger and sought not only to destroy Mordecai, but all of the Jews in the land.

Haman's first step was to cast lots to determine a date for the mass extermination. His second act was to approach the king with a false report concerning the Jewish people, and to present them as a danger and threat to the kingdom. He urged for a decree to be issued to order the death of all Jews. Haman offered to personally put ten thousand talents of silver into the royal treasury for those who carried out this edict.

King Ahasuerus sealed the death decree with his signet ring and in doing so sentenced thousands of innocent men, women, and children to death at the altar of Haman's wickedness.

Mordecai was dedicated, consecrated and connected to the Lord. He was not only in relationship *with* Him, but was set apart *to* Him—and would not bend or bow his knee to any other so-called god.

The death decree was sent throughout the land that on the

165

thirteenth day of the twelfth month, all Jews were to be killed. The king and Haman sat down to drink, but the people of Shushan were perplexed concerning why such a thing was to be done.

"FOR SUCH A TIME AS THIS"

How we handle difficult days can be an enormous challenge.

Times had grown progressively worse for Mordecai who was looking for brighter days for his people, though they had not come. In response to what was taking place, and knowing he was the main object of Haman's hatred, Mordecai tore his clothes and put on sackcloth with ashes.

He went to the king's gate, yet could go no further because no one was allowed to enter wearing sackcloth. In every province there was great mourning among the Jews with fasting, weeping and wailing.

Esther also grieved and sent fresh clothing to Mordecai, but he refused them. Mordecai knew it was time for war—not a conflict with spears or swords, he was taking their cause to the Lord.

As we approach our best days, we will be faced with some major decisions. When Mordecai rejected the clothing sent by Esther, she sent Hatach, one of the king's chamberlains, to discover the reason for his behavior. He told Hatach all that had happened to him and of the plans and decree Haman had orchestrated.

Next, Mordecai sent word to Esther, charging her to go to the king and make request to him concerning the edict. Esther sent a message back to Mordecai that whoever entered the king's court uninvited could be put to death. If the king did not raise his scepter to approve a person's approach, that person would be killed.

Mordecai warned her not to think she would escape if the decree was carried out. He told her if she failed to act, deliverance for their people would come from another source, but her father's house would be destroyed. Then he made this profound statement: *"...who knoweth whether thou art come to the kingdom for such a time as this?"* (Esther 4:14).

TIME FOR A DECISION

We need more believers like Mordecai—those who will stand firm for the Lord's cause and do whatever it takes to defeat the enemy. God is looking for men and women who are not easily discouraged, who know, one way or another, He will work everything out for their good.

Like Esther, we are here for such a time as this. We cannot afford to leave the work for others when we are capable of accomplishing the task. Our greatest and perhaps *only* impact will be made during these days because the Lord placed us here for this moment.

Esther got word back to Mordecai telling him to gather all of the Jews in Shushan and fast for her three days and nights. She and her maidens were also going to fast. She would then personally go to the king and speak to him about the matter. Esther said, "If I perish, I perish."

She made a major decision that would ultimately bring the Israelites their best days.

THE CHOICE IS YOURS

Decision-making is a process which is properly arrived at after all the factors involved have been prayerfully considered. For example, in marriage, the selection of a spouse is made not only after falling in love, but by considering the character, actions, deeds and accomplishments of an individual. Without facts or knowledge, the basis of a choice is questionable.

Esther took the situation to God, but she also looked at the details. She considered her people, the impact of the decree, her position as queen, the law concerning presenting oneself before the king, the threat to her life and the fact the Lord had placed her there for this particular time. She also thought about the desire of her God, and fasted for His intervention.

Decisions can produce our best or worst days—and anything in between. They can make life enjoyable or miserable, determine success or failure and the rate at which we achieve. This is why it is vital we always seek the Lord's guidance before making any choice.

Esther, after fasting and praying, made the decision to go before the king. She put on her royal apparel and stood in the inner court of the palace. The king was seated upon his royal throne.

When he saw Esther, she obtained his favor and he held out the golden scepter which was in his hand. She drew near to her husband and touched the top of the scepter. Then King Ahasuerus asked, *"What wilt thou, queen Esther? and what is thy request? it shall be even given thee to the half of the kingdom"* (Esther 5:3).

What a great feeling when we make a major decision and immediately see it was the right one. However, remember Esther and Mordecai had already consulted the Lord. It is good to be directed by the Father, because when we make a move, it will be according to His design.

GOD'S REWARD PROCESS

We must have a plan of achievement.

Esther requested the king join her for a banquet the next day—and that Haman be present. He agreed. It is sometimes necessary for us to go on the offensive and attack the enemy, rather than always assuming a defensive posture.

When Haman was informed of his upcoming meeting with the royal couple, he was joyful and filled with expectation, boasting to his friends about his promotion and possessions. Still, Haman despised Mordecai.

As Haman passed the king's gate, Mordecai did not stand up, neither did he move aside for him. Haman's wife and friends suggested a gallows be made, fifty cubits high, and that he speak to the king about hanging Mordecai there. Haman agreed and had the gallows constructed.

God's plan of reward is underway!

On the night before the banquet, the king was restless and could not sleep. He commanded that the book of the chronicles be brought to him. He saw recorded in the pages the account of Mordecai's report of the plan to harm him. When Mordecai first reported the incident, the king did not compensate him. However, the reward was underway and would soon be delivered.

Ahasuerus did not simply wake up; the Lord aroused him.

The king asked, *"What honour and dignity hath been done to Mordecai for this? Then said the king's servants that ministered unto him, There is nothing done for him"* (Esther 6:3).

Haman was arriving with plans to speak to the king and obtain permission to hang Mordecai on the gallows he had built. However, the king asked the first question: "What should be done unto the man in whom the king delights?"

Haman thought Ahasuerus was making reference to him, but he was actually speaking of Mordecai. Haman responded, "The king should dress that person in royal apparel and place him upon one of the palace horses." He suggested that a crown be placed upon his head and he be paraded through the streets on horseback.

The king told Haman to prepare all of his suggested honor for Mordecai, and not to fail in any aspect. What a shock to Haman!

While the enemy seeks to bury us, the Lord blesses us. Haman sought to destroy Mordecai, yet God delivered him.

Haman did all the king ordered, then ran to his house crying, with his head covered. His wife and wisemen said to him, *"If Mordecai be of the seed of the Jews, before whom thou hast begun to fall, thou shalt not prevail against him, but shalt surely fall before him"* (Esther 6:13).

THE TURN-AROUND

Our best days will surely arrive.

The king, Esther, and Haman were at the banquet when Esther informed her husband that a plot was underway to slaughter both her and all of her people. The king wanted to know who was behind such a scheme. Esther replied that the adversary and enemy was none other than the wicked Haman.

In his anger, the king rose up and went into the palace garden to think. Haman begged Esther to save his life—falling on the bed where the queen was.

Ahasuerus returned and saw Haman on the bed and said, *"Will he force the queen also before me in the house?"* (Esther 7:8).

One of the servants told the king about the gallows Haman had constructed for Mordecai. In an amazing turn of events, King Ahasuerus gave the order to hang Haman on the very gallows he had prepared for Mordecai.

Our best days are coming and no foe can stop them. Many have already been defeated and rendered ineffective. Enemy plans have been reversed.

The king cancelled the decree of Haman to destroy the Jews.

- What the enemy means for evil, God will use for our good.
- What is meant to kill will give life.
- What is meant to harm will help.
- What is meant to tear down will build up.
- What is meant to stop us will propel us higher.
- What is meant to bring sorrow will bring joy.
- What is meant to sit us down will cause us to dance.
- What is meant to have us pity ourselves will cause us to praise our God.
- What is meant to have us wallow in pain will cause us to worship in gain.

The time-frame for our destruction has been cancelled.

Haman plotted to have all the Jews destroyed on the thirteenth day of the twelfth month, but God had another plan. Instead, on that very date, a new decree was published allowing the Jews to defend themselves in every province.

The enemy's defeat will usher in our best days.

Haman's house was given to Esther and the king presented the ring he had taken from Haman to Mordecai. He also set Mordecai over the house of Haman—and from that moment on he was allowed total access to the palace.

Mordecai was now dressed in the royal apparel of blue and white, with a crown of gold and garments of fine linen and purple. The people of the land both feared and honored him because he was exalted in the king's house, and his fame spread abroad.

WHAT A FUTURE!

If you want a preview—plus an assurance—of what is just around the corner, open the pages of God's Word.

Our suffering will be no more.

"But the God of all grace, who hath called us unto his eternal glory by Christ Jesus, after that ye have suffered a while, make you perfect..." (1 Peter 5:10).

Our nights of crying will be over.

"For his anger endureth but for a moment; in his favour is life: weeping may endure for a night, but joy cometh in the morning" (Psalm 30:5).

Our burdens will pass.

"Cast thy burden upon the Lord, and he shall sustain thee: he shall never suffer the righteous to be moved" (Psalm 5:22).

Our enemy will be defeated.

"...When the enemy shall come in like a flood, the Spirit of the Lord shall lift up a standard against him" (Isaiah 59:19).

I know who I am and what the Lord has shown me about my future. The reason I can make it through the present is because I can see tomorrow. It is my faith which provides me with the necessary strength to handle whatever comes my way. My struggles are temporary; they will pass.

I pray you will take the words of this book and apply them to your life—starting today.

Learn to look beyond where you are at this moment to the glorious place God has prepared. The potential the Lord has placed within you has no limit. Open your heart to His vision and act on His dream.

Arise every morning expecting the best—then give it your all! You can do it!

NOTES

FOR A COMPLETE LIST OF BOOKS
AND MEDIA RESOURCES BY
DR. JEROME STOKES,
CONTACT:

CHURCH OF THE REDEEMED OF THE LORD
4321 OLD YORK ROAD
BALTIMORE, MD 21212

PHONE 1-866-THE LAMP (843-5267)